THEIR VOICE MATTERS

Child Custody Solutions for Effective Co-Parenting

Copyright ©2020 by Dameon K. Wroe
Another **EP**® Publishing Company

All rights reserved. All materials and/or supporting text written in this book are the original work *and* creation of the author, and are protected by applicable copyright laws on file with the Library of Congress Copyright Office. Any photocopying, reproductions, publications, alterations or duplications of this book and the information contained herein, without the author's *or* the publisher's expressed written consent, is a violation of applicable laws. It is equally a violation of applicable laws to copy, post, re-post, print or otherwise transfer any text from this book onto any social media platforms, for *any* reason whatsoever, without the author's *or* the publisher's expressed written consent.

To book any of our authors for public speaking engagements, appearances, book signing events or workshops, address all inquiries in writing to:

Another **EP**® Publishing Company
Post Office Box 300
Walnut, CA 91788-0300
or by email at: anothereppublishingcompany@gmail.com

Cover Design and Layout: DAEdesign

Printed in the United States
9 8 7 6 5 4 3 2 1

ISBN#: 978-0-9740685-3-4

The characters in this book are fictitious, but the scenarios depicted in this book are based on true, real life events pertaining to no one individual in particular. If you purchased this book without a cover, you should know that this book is stolen property. It was reported as "unsold" or "destroyed" to the publisher and neither the author nor the publisher has received any payments for this "stripped book."

Table of Contents

1	The Onset of Separation and Divorce	1
2	What to Expect in Court	15
3	Suck it Up!	31
4	Shaping Your Child's Future	45
5	Choose Your Advisors Carefully	55
6	Setting Traps for the Other Parent	67
7	Understanding Their Language	79
8	In Times of Need	97
9	Always Choose Your Child	117

Introduction

This book is an educational, family court resource guide designed for the purpose of teaching you about the modern day dynamics of effective co-parenting principles in today's society. As history continues to disruptively repeat itself, we are constantly being forced to witness the aftermath of relationships gone wrong, and the innocent children who are oftentimes caught in the cross-fire of divorce and separation!

Whether you were ordered by a court of law to complete this book, it was recommended to you by a social worker or you just made a personal decision to purchase it on your own because you're striving to be a better parent, the wealth of knowledge that you will gain by reading this book will take your co-parenting skills to the next level.

This book is, without a doubt, going to challenge you on more levels than you're even prepared to imagine right now but, since your ultimate goal is to be a better parent or co-parent, you will see that it's going to be well worth the sacrifices that you may have to make along the way. Do not take your opportunity to read this book lightly by any means.

Unlike anything else you've ever done in your life as a parent, this is an opportunity for you to grow into a level of parental maturity that maybe you've never been taught before. This is an opportunity for you to really reflect on some things you may have done wrong that you don't wish to do any longer. Maybe reading this book was just the wake-up call you needed to save you from getting your children taken away from you or losing what minimal level of custody you are currently enjoying.

By the time you finish reading this book, only YOU will be able to decide if you have learned anything from it or not. Only YOU will be able to decide if you're going to keep on doing things the way you've always done them, or if you're going to only do what's in the best interests of your child.

As you navigate your way through this book, you may find similarities in these stories and scenarios that match your current situation that you are battling in your own co-parenting relationship. However, when you find that you have become emotionally charged by what you are reading, that very emotion becomes the evidence needed to identify the fact that there's a connection between this book and your life that allows you to see that change is needed much sooner rather than much later.

Make no mistake about it – this book is going to challenge how much you really love your child! This book is going to challenge if YOU are the parent who should have joint custody,

INTRODUCTION

minimal custody or no custody at all. This book is definitely going to challenge your ability to make favorable, sound decisions for *your child*. This book is going to call into question if being a parent is all about YOU or all about your child.

Reading this book is going to be unlike any emotional or psychological rollercoaster you've ever been on. There are going to be many different, real-life scenarios sprinkled throughout this book that will make you smile, that will make you laugh, that will make you angry, that will make you want to seek revenge and that will make you want to cry.

When you come to a part in this book that you feel is guiding you to the dark corners of your mind, stay focused on the message… because the message is the *light*! Your manhood is going to be tested all throughout this book. Your womanhood is going to be tested all throughout this book. Your **integrity**[1] is going to be tested all throughout this book. Your level of maturity is going to be tested all throughout this book. Your conflict resolution skills are going to be tested all throughout this book. Your character, your ego and your ability to remain calm and cordial with your co-parent is all going to be tested throughout this book.

Whether or not you pass those tests depends on your mindset and your willingness to apply the principles, techniques and recommendations that will be offered to you in this book.

This book was inspired by each and every mistake that I

---

1 Firm adherence to a code of especially moral or artistic values: incorruptibility.

personally made as a parent during the time that I was also going through an extremely bitter and chaotic divorce. It was also inspired by a wide array of relationship fails that I either witnessed or learned about from other people. When I filed for divorce, my children were still very young. At the onset of my own divorce filing, my ex-wife and I had initially agreed to remain cordial with one another for the sake of our children. As time went on, and multiple circumstances had compromised our vows, and the way we communicated, I made it my feverish mission to get back at her every chance I got, for the purpose of showing her that I was in control, not her… and for making insignificant things in her life more of a priority than our children. I made it my daily priority to make sure that I made her feel as inferior and as defeated as possible.

For every time that I was able to make her life a living hell, I ultimately came to the realization that I was also making my *own* life a living hell. Through the ongoing encouragement and moral support that I received from my family and friends, I started to see that it was virtually impossible for ME to control HER actions. Once I finally accepted the fact that I could only change myself, while reflecting on how I was *choosing* to negatively respond to her, things got so much better for me – more importantly, things got better for our children.

This book is also inspired by the mistakes that I wish I never made as a father, even long after my divorce was over. I realize that there's no training manual for raising children, but I also realize that every day that we are allowed to wake up and see another day is another chance to right our wrongs and be a

INTRODUCTION

better person *today* than we were *yesterday!*

As you prepare to dive further into this book, this is the time where you need to make a concrete commitment to keep an open mind from beginning to end. Though the actual names of the people in the scenarios of this book are fictional, the actual scenarios depicted will be based on real life occurrences.

Rather than focusing on the problematic and **dysfunctional**[2] events that will be disclosed in each chapter, focus on the positive lessons that can be learned by merely reading about what someone else had to go through just so that YOU could benefit from the lesson or experience.

If your goal is to use this book to try and find fault in the other co-parent, then you have already failed and missed the lessons to be learned here. If your goal is to use this book to always have "**one-up**"[3] over the other co-parent then, again, you have already failed and have missed the lessons to be learned throughout this book. If you decide to allow your stubbornness to dictate and control the most critical aspects of your decision-making methods then, one of these days, you will find yourself standing before a family law judge or commissioner who can make court orders that will in no way be favorable for you.

Think of this book as being on a very long road trip! When you are on a long road trip, you oftentimes get uncomfortable when you've been sitting in the same position for prolonged

---

2 Characterized by or exhibiting dysfunction; not functioning properly; marked by impaired or abnormal functioning.

3 Having an advantage over someone.

periods of time. You also get leg cramps, your back muscles tighten up, there's very little room to stretch and sometimes there's no one to help you drive those long distances when you're exhausted and feel like you can't go on any further.

When you've been on such a long journey such as this, you need to stop and rest so that you do not become too fatigued to continue your journey safely. If this has ever happened to you, at some point, you eventually exited the freeway and pulled into a **rest area**.[4] Pulling over at a rest area gives you a chance to get out of your car and stretch your legs, it allows you to take a water and/or restroom break, and it also gives you a brief opportunity to close your eyes and take a short mental break as well.

As you move further and further into reading this book, you will see that there will be *mental rest areas* for you to stop and take a mental break. The rest areas throughout this book will also be your intimate moments of accountability and reflection to identify your strengths and weaknesses along your journey of effective parenting and/or co-parenting. These mental rest areas will eventually be your saving grace because, as you journey through this book and start to unpack your thoughts, you will learn more about yourself than you've ever taken the time to notice before.

As you will soon learn, there will always be voices running through your mind along your journey of being a parent and

---

[4] An area adjacent to a highway at which restrooms and refreshments are usually available.

INTRODUCTION

doing your best to raise your child, but you have to be mature enough to know which voice to listen to. Are you going to listen to your own selfish, stubborn voice? Are you going to deny *your* wants and desires to listen to the voice of reason? Whichever voice you choose to listen to, just remember the most important fact that you will ever read in this book, it's not *your voice* that matters… it's ***their** voice* that matters!

THEIR VOICE MATTERS

Child Custody Solutions for Effective Co-Parenting

CHAPTER 1

The Onset of Separation and Divorce

Fellas: Do you remember where you were and who you were with when you first laid eyes on your girlfriend, spouse or significant other? Do you remember that overwhelming feeling of desire you felt when the possibility of you becoming her man seemed so real?

How about the adrenaline that rushed through your body when you were building up the courage to step to her and ask her out on a date? Remember that? Do you recall that first impression she made on you when you saw her in that sexy outfit or that flashy sports car? More than likely, when she first stepped into your focus, you said to yourself or your buddies, "If I could just get her phone number and go out on one date with her… the rest would be history! I would make her mine and hold onto her forever."

At first glance, you immediately loved everything about

her. You loved the fact that she was obviously very attractive. You loved the fact that she appeared to be very self-confident by how she carried herself. You were so impressed with how every hair on her head fell right into place, exactly where it needed to be in order for you to identify her as the perfect woman for *you*.

This all seemed too real to be true. Everything about this woman seemed like it was right out of a fairytale. She was the perfect height, her hair and nails were on point, she was wearing her clothes in such a way that gave you the best glance of her figure and, to top it all off, she was all alone… so it was a good sign that she might be single. Without any further hesitation or reservations, you made your move and asked her for her phone number. To your surprise, she gave you her phone number and the ball was in your court!

Ladies: Do you remember where you were at and what you were doing when you were first approached by the man who made you want to go home and write in your diary or journal before you went to bed? Do you recall him being so handsome and **debonair**[5] that, when he walked by you and got only a short distance away from you, you turned around to do a double-take so that you could admire his masculinity just one more time before he faded out of focus?

Does your memory take you back to the day when a girlfriend introduced him to you at a friend's party and you just couldn't ignore his sexy eyes or his macho stature? Maybe you met him at church and, when church was over, you walked

---

5 Suave; urbane.

CHAPTER 1: THE ONSET OF SEPARATION AND DIVORCE

up to greet him with a handshake and he ended up giving you a tight "church hug" and a "holy kiss" on the cheek unexpectedly! Being the reserved, mild-mannered, fun, yet reserved woman you might be, you did not want to let this piece of **eye candy**[6] pass you by, so you talked to him a little bit about the type of work you do and handed him one of your business cards.

Scenario #1

This chapter is based on the story of two people that we will refer to as Raymond and Myra, to protect the identities of the actual persons who may or may not be depicted in these scenarios. Raymond and Myra met each other at church during a church function and started dating after just a few months of getting to know each other. Myra already had a three-year-old daughter from a previous relationship but, at the time, Raymond did not have any children. Luckily for Myra, and her daughter Angelica, Raymond was extremely family-oriented and prided himself on his reputation for loving children so much. It was just a matter of time before Myra began to notice that her daughter Angelica was beginning to grow on Raymond more and more as time went by.

Raymond and Myra did everything together – there were not too many things that could keep them apart. Their relationship got off to a pretty amazing start, to say the least. Compared to the life she once had with Angelica's father, Myra

---

6 Something superficially attractive to look at.

was at the happiest place in her life that she had ever been since she started dating Raymond.

At the time they first met, Myra was a single mother who had moved back home to live with her parents, due to previously being in a physically abusive relationship with Angelica's father shortly after Angelica was born. Because they had a zero tolerance for the physical abuse that Myra was dealing with, her parents let her come back home, but with two conditions.

The first condition was that Myra had to either be working full-time or going to school, so that she wasn't just sitting around her parent's house being counter-productive and lazy. The second condition was that she could only stay at home for two years before her parents would eventually require her to move out and get her own place. Despite the demands of living under her parent's roof, Myra did not let a few house rules stand in the way of falling in love with Raymond. Whenever he told her that he was going to come pick her up for a date, Raymond was never late.

Though there are a lot of men out there in today's society who do not do this very often for the woman they love, Raymond would always open and close the car door for Myra. He would always open up doors for her at restaurants, at church and virtually any other place that they went together. Most importantly, he would always have Myra back at her parent's house before midnight, as those were also part of the house rules while she and her young daughter were allowed to live there; Raymond respected that. Raymond was not the average type of boyfriend; he was every *good woman's* dream!

CHAPTER 1: THE ONSET OF SEPARATION AND DIVORCE

He was an educated family man who also prided himself on protecting his loved ones from any hurt, harm or danger. Like Myra, he was very religious and believed strongly in always making an honest effort to attend church services on a regular basis.

Whenever someone made Myra upset, Raymond was always there to shield her from anyone who was causing Myra's safety or mental health to feel **compromised**[7]. During their quality time that they would often spend together, Myra admired Raymond's unique ability to be that disciplinarian figure to her daughter but then, in a matter of seconds, he could go right back to being the fun-loving, charming and lovable man he had always been from day one. For Myra, this was yet another sign that she had found the right man to be in her life. Although they had quite a bit in common, there were some qualities about Myra that would not surface for years to come.

In the early stages of their relationship, prior to their mutual agreement to exclusively date only each other, Myra had all the qualities and characteristics of a certified **introvert**[8]. Even after church services were over, Myra could almost always be found retreating straight to her car to leave while other members were roaming around socializing and greeting each other; she was a very **standoffish**[9] type of person. She came from a very

---

7 Made vulnerable (as to attack or misuse) by unauthorized access, revelation, or exposure.

8 A reserved or shy person who enjoys spending time alone.

9 Somewhat cold and reserved.

religious family upbringing and *appeared* to have a very good head on her shoulders. Raymond was particularly impressed with the fact that Myra *appeared* to be a very good mother to her daughter Angelica, and the fact that she was also going to school part-time at a local community college to secure a better future for her and her daughter. Since Raymond was nearly five years older than Myra, his age and his level of maturity made her feel so much more secure in her relationship with him. In Myra's eyes, he was all that she had been needing… and more!

As Raymond and Myra's relationship continued to blossom like a beautiful, red rose, they were both about to experience things that they would remember for the rest of their lives. After dating for a few short years, Raymond decided within himself that he was ready to take his relationship with Myra to the next level and transition from *boyfriend* to *husband*.

Being the charming, affectionate and fun-loving man that he was, Raymond strategically planned out the perfect weekend to complete his mission. On a particular Friday evening, Raymond met up with Myra and gave her some money to go and get her hair and nails done on the following day. The next day, Myra was so happy and so flattered, that she could not stop telling all of her friends about the gesture of true love that Raymond had just demonstrated towards her… again. Once Raymond had confirmed that Myra was with her girlfriends, well into her weekend, the stage was set. Executing his master plan, Raymond drove over to Myra's parent's house to ask for their daughter's hand in marriage.

This was a very dynamic turning-point in Raymond and

CHAPTER 1: THE ONSET OF SEPARATION AND DIVORCE

Myra's life because, prior to entertaining the idea of marriage, they had both been through some very hard times in their own individual lives.

Prior to meeting Myra, Raymond had just been released from prison after serving 21 months for DUI, while Myra had been struggling to get on her feet financially and get her own place for her and her daughter. While Raymond was incarcerated, he ended up losing his home because there was no one to keep his bills paid while he was away; he had been temporarily staying with a family member.

As for Myra, her parents were growing increasingly irritated that she did not appear to be aggressively looking for her own apartment, and they felt she was being lazy and wanted her out. This tense and consistently awkward arrangement was beginning to back Myra into a dark corner of inevitable uncertainty.

After sitting down with Myra's parents for the better half of about two hours, Raymond was interrogated and put on notice at the same time. Myra's parents wanted to know why Raymond loved Myra so much that he wanted to spend the rest of his life with her. Raymond was noticeably proud to share with them that Myra made his world turn on so many levels that he felt like he just could not live without her and Angelica. He loved how much of a dedicated mother she was to her child. He also made it crystal clear that he adored Myra's daughter, Angelica, as if she were his own child.

Disclosing these facts truly sealed the deal between Raymond and Myra's parents and, when they felt that they had finally heard enough, Raymond left Myra's parent's house with their full blessing and support of taking her hand in marriage.

Since the soon-to-be newlyweds were both pretty much in "survival mode," they had some life-changing choices to make with very little time to spare for adequate family planning. If their relationship was ever going to experience taking a "leap of faith," now was the time for them to jump! Approximately one year later, Raymond and Myra were finally husband and wife.

The first year of their marriage was nothing shy of **blissful**.[10] Anyone that knew Raymond knew how much of a hard-working, dedicated family man he was. He had a long-standing reputation for being a family man who did not put very many things before the love of his family. Raymond was a very loyal person, with regard to the relationships that he had built over the years, and he was especially loyal and dedicated to his new bride. For the most part, Raymond and Myra were two peas in a pod; inseparable, to say the least.

Also during their first year of marriage, the couple's first child, Cameron, was born. Everything was quickly coming together for the new family of four. Raymond had finally graduated with his master's degree in communication, and Myra had just been promoted on her job where she worked as an Administrative Assistant for a very well established corporation. It didn't take long for Raymond and Myra's marriage to become an open display of what a happy life looked like but, unfortunately, after being married for only three short

---

10 Full of, marked by, or causing complete happiness.

CHAPTER 1: THE ONSET OF SEPARATION AND DIVORCE

years, a laundry list of **recurring**[11] problems began to take an unexpected and overwhelming toll on Raymond and Myra's vows.

The Writing on the Wall

The dynamics of *life* and *relationships* are a lot like the dynamics of driving. When you have driven to a particular place enough times, you know exactly how to get there without relying on any written or GPS navigated directions. Not only do you know how to get there, you also know of at least one or two shortcuts to take if traffic happens to be unexpectedly bad. If you were not paying attention to the signs along the highway while driving to your destination, it would be just a matter of time before you realized that you were lost and had no idea where you were going.

Before we go any further, I want to take your mind as far back as humanly possible to see if you can identify the most critical factors that led you to believe that your relationship or your marriage was inevitably running the end of its course.

Do you recall the times when your spouse or co-parent would always rush home as soon as the workday was over, just to hurry up and spend time with you? Do you recall all of the workdays where you hardly got any work done at the office because you and your spouse or co-parent were too busy texting, emailing or calling each other obsessively because you

---

11 Occurring repeatedly; happening or appearing multiple times.

missed each other so much? Do you remember how you felt deep down in your soul as your wedding day got closer, or when it got closer to the day that your child was about to be born?

Can you remember how excited you felt to learn that your leave of absence from work was finally approved, so that you could spend the first few months of your new baby's life with them every day? At what point in time did you sense that things in your relationship were changing for the worse?

Was it the time when you noticed that your spouse or co-parent held your hand noticeably different? Was it the time that you noticed your spouse was *"suddenly"* spending far more time *"at work"* rather than coming straight home to be with you and the rest of the family as they once did in the beginning? Was it the time when you noticed that you stopped getting those long hugs and sweet kisses from your spouse or co-parent when they had finally made it home? When did you *really* start to notice that things between the two of you just weren't the same anymore?

Was it the morning that you woke up and went into the kitchen, only to discover that your spouse or co-parent had put *their* name on certain food items that *they* had bought, as their way of telling you to leave it alone? Was it when you noticed that your spouse or co-parent had washed all of the dirty laundry in the house… except yours? Was it when you came home from a long day at work to a house that smelled like your spouse or co-parent had just cooked an amazing dinner, only to find out that they cooked just enough food for themselves and

CHAPTER 1: THE ONSET OF SEPARATION AND DIVORCE

didn't leave any for you?

I'll bet you noticed things started to go sideways when you discovered that your spouse or co-parent had taken their name off of the joint checking/savings account and opened up an account of their own so that you no longer had any knowledge about how much money they did or did not have in the bank. No? Am I close yet? I got it! Did you finally notice that your relationship was doomed when you realized that the passionate intimacy that you once both shared had come to a screeching halt? I knew that was it! Or was it that time when you made your spouse or co-parent stay at home alone with the kids so that you could stay out in the streets all hours of the night and then come back home whenever you wanted to – and without any explanation whatsoever as to where you had been?

If you have found yourself being able to relate to *any* of the situations that were just described, these are probably some of the trigger-points that eventually made you become enraged and eventually prompted you to fly off the handle. These are just a few of the most commonly recognizable trigger-points that can make any reasonable person come unglued or simply SNAP! The above signs of dysfunction in a relationship which has become toxic for children are classified as *the writing on the wall*.

The onset of separation and divorce typically creates so much hostility and violence between co-parents that, throughout the separation or divorce process, the parties seemingly forget that they even have children together! When couples allow themselves to become irate and enraged to the point that all they desire to do is get back at each other for what they feel the other parent did wrong, then the "mutual combat mentality" becomes the foundation for extremely long periods of counter-productive communications!

Once things have gone *this* far and have gotten *this* out of hand, it becomes the very behavior that always places the innocent children in the cross-fire of the parents who are only focused on hurting one another and getting back at each other for reasons that shouldn't even matter any longer.

This chapter *and* this book are designed to help you focus on what role you're *truly* playing in the parenting or co-parenting process. I want to challenge you to <u>change your mindset</u> so that greater things can happen *for your child*, not so that greater things can happen for YOU! When you finally get to a place where you can see the value of greater things happening for your children, great things are going to happen for you by default! If you keep doing what you've always done, you're going to keep on getting what you've always gotten.

This is the part of the book where you learn that, if you do not change some of your ways, you may very well find yourself losing complete custody of your children… if you haven't lost it already! On the other hand, if you have always had very little custody or no custody at all to begin with, then the valuable lessons that you learn *AND APPLY* from this book can possibly turn your circumstances around so that you can start spending more and more time with your children, which is what should matter to you the most.

Rather than learning from YOUR mistakes, learn from

CHAPTER 1: THE ONSET OF SEPARATION AND DIVORCE

the mistakes of the characters in this book as you continue reading. In order for you to learn from your own mistakes, you must first go through the unforgiving process of getting into enough trouble with the law – and hope that you are able to get yourself out of it. Do not put yourself in a position to end up in trouble with the law just so that you can learn a lesson from the experience.

If you choose to remain stubborn, and decide that you want to do things your own way, rather than the right way, then you are establishing a terrible reputation for yourself in the eyes of any family court before you even get there to have your case heard! **DO NOT** do that to yourself and, most importantly, **DO NOT** do that to your children, because they will be affected by every single decision that you either make or refuse to make. Your children are counting on you to make the right decisions for *their* benefit, so choose wisely. Good luck!

CHAPTER 2

What to Expect in Court

Aren't you excited that you are finally about to get your day in court soon? You have FINALLY made it to this point and have gained your opportunity to step into the courtroom arena to take advantage of securing your legal separation or divorce. With all of the concrete evidence that you have to show how terrible the other parent has been during your relationship, the courthouse doors cannot possibly open up soon enough! You can't WAIT for YOUR VOICE to be heard!

As your first court date rapidly approaches, it is reasonably expected that your anxiety is probably all over the place about what to expect on your big day in court. For days and weeks now, you have been going over all of your paperwork, exhibits and other **evidentiary**[12] documents, and you can't wait for your

---

12 Being, relating to or affording evidence; conducted so that evidence may be presented.

chance to get the judge so upset at your spouse or co-parent, that the judge scolds the other co-parent in front of everyone in the courtroom!

Since you have so many friends, family members and concerned associates that are eager to show their **allegiance**[13] to you by helping you come up with ways to make the other parent look bad in court, you have already spent a great deal of your time rehearsing what you think is the most damaging information you are going to share first in court.

Before you go into court with that kind of mindset, let me save you a great deal of pain, heartache, time, money and emotional torture. No matter what type of proof or evidence you think you have to convince the court of everything wrong that the other parent did to you during the relationship, THE COURT DOES NOT CARE ABOUT ANY OF IT! In case you missed something, let me say it to you one more time. No matter what type of proof or evidence you think you have to convince the court of everything wrong that the other parent did to you during the relationship, THE. COURT. DOES. NOT. CARE!

The only thing that the court is concerned about is what's in the best interest of your child – nothing more, nothing less and nothing else! Never, at any time, should you go into a courtroom amped up and eager to tell the court about everything that the other parent *is* doing or *has* done to upset you or make you angry during the separation or divorce process. If you walk into

---

13 Devotion or loyalty to a person, group or cause.

CHAPTER 2: WHAT TO EXPECT IN COURT

a court of law with that type of demeanor or **disposition**[14], you will end up making a complete fool of yourself and ultimately embarrass yourself in front of everyone else in the courtroom that may have the present ability to listen to the details of your case. Once your case is called before the court, there is no such thing as privacy!

You must remember to keep in mind that the judge, or commissioner, has already read and reviewed your case-file before you even get to court. So, by the time you actually make it into the courtroom and go before the court, they do not want to hear the *in-person version* of everything that you have already put in writing when you filed your initial paperwork. In a family law matter that involves legal separation or divorce, the person who files their papers *first* is known throughout the duration of the case as the **Petitioner**[15].

Once the *petitioner* files their case with the court, the next step is to have the other party served with a copy of the papers that were filed by the *petitioner*. When this happens, the other party is referred to as the **Respondent**[16] throughout the duration of the case. Based on the specific dynamics that are directly related to your particular family law matter (court case), the court has the discretion to make a wide variety of orders concerning the terms and conditions of your legal separation, divorce or child custody matters.

---

14 Prevailing tendency, mood or inclination.
15 A person who asks to have a legal case decided by a court.
16 An answering party in a proceeding in juvenile court or family court.

A few of the most common orders that the court can make include, but are not limited to:

- Spousal Support
- Child Support
- Child Custody
- Parenting Time / Visitation
- Division of Assets
- Alimony

Generally speaking, the courts try to make the kind of rulings that are reasonably fair for both the *petitioner and* the *respondent* but, even before that happens, the court's primary focus and duty is to make orders and rulings that are in the absolute best interests of any minor children… because *their voice* matters! Since neither of them had ever been through the divorce process before, both Raymond and Myra were in for a very rude awakening.

Scenario #2

The circumstances that ultimately led to Raymond filing for divorce were the driving force behind the bitterness, resentment, hatred and anger that fueled his divorce proceedings. Of the many diverse reasons that couples get divorced, there are several common reasons that are at the top of the list. The most

CHAPTER 2: WHAT TO EXPECT IN COURT

common reasons that people get divorced include, but are not limited to: financial irresponsibility, ongoing communication problems, **infidelity**[17], domestic violence and even mental or emotional abuse. As luck would have it, infidelity was also what led Raymond to file for divorce.

Since he was more of a rational thinker than Myra, Raymond was initially able to persuade Myra to work with him to make their divorce process as painless as possible. Approximately two months before Raymond had actually filed for divorce, he found evidence that his wife had been seeing another man. Understandably so, this enraged Raymond so much that he knew he had to move out, or risk ending up in jail for not being able to control his emotions.

Since Raymond was not a violent person by nature, his plan for maintaining his anger was demonstrated by the fact that he *chose* to make a daily decision to make Myra's life a living hell for what he felt she did to destroy the trust in their marriage. Needless to say, his decision to conduct himself in this manner would later prove to be something that he would ultimately regret.

At their very first court appearance, tensions between Raymond and Myra were nothing shy of obvious. While Myra entered into the courtroom with only a large manila folder containing a few court documents, Raymond showed up ready for battle. He entered the courtroom with a briefcase, a video camera that showed proof of Myra cheating on him, and two

---

17 Unfaithfulness to a moral obligation; disloyalty.

small boxes of papers that he intended to show to the judge that supported his claims of Myra's infidelity. After Raymond had finally finished unloading all of his **allegations**[18] against Myra onto the court, it was her turn to vent.

Myra tried her best to defend herself against Raymond's embarrassing allegation that she had cheated on him with another man during their marriage. She rambled on and on to the court about how Raymond stalked her on a regular basis and would oftentimes show up at her job trying to get her fired by causing a scene and provoking her to engage in heated arguments. It didn't take long for the court to see that Raymond and Myra's childish, self-centered concerns had *nothing* to do with the welfare and benefit of their innocent and defenseless children… and the court put a very abrupt end to their courtroom shenanigans!

Due to their obvious lack of concern for the well-being of their children's physical, emotional and psychological health, the court was extremely disgusted with both Raymond and Myra's behavior. This is the very type of counter-productive behaviors that oftentimes drown out the silent screams of the children who, by the actions of their parents, will slowly start to feel as though they are the reason for the problems that exist between their parents. Even though many children who are caught in the middle of bitter divorces cannot verbally articulate how they are feeling about the separation of their parents, they

---

18 An assertion unsupported and by implication regarded as unsupportable.

CHAPTER 2: WHAT TO EXPECT IN COURT

communicate their feelings by acting them out in a variety of different ways, as you will see in the chapters ahead.

As a parent who has been hurt in some way by a co-parent, it is a natural feeling and emotion to want to go into a courtroom to defend yourself and your position, relating to the separation or divorce with your own interests at heart. The courts are very aware that couples who are preparing to go their separate ways are eager to come to court to voice their concerns about what led up to their separation. However, what you always need to remember is that it's not *your voice* that matters to the court, it's all about hearing what the needs of your children are – because *their voice* matters!

When you first begin making your initial court appearances, the objective of the court is to reach a mutual resolution between you and your co-parent as soon as humanly possible so that effective court orders can be made that will determine how you and your co-parent will work together to care for your children until the children reach the legal age of 18 years old.

Your first few court appearances are not the time for you to start bringing in your personal file cabinets filled with evidence against the other parent so that you can celebrate any potential punishment that the court might hand down to them. Your first few court appearances are strictly for the purposes of allowing the court to see what agreements have already been established between you and your co-parent, and how the court may need to intervene to make orders that pertain to everything else that you and your co-parent cannot seem to come to an agreement on.

Once it becomes obvious to the court that you and the other parent have unresolved conflicts pertaining to issues related to your case, the court will most likely order you and the other parent to attend **mediation**[19].

The purpose of mediation is to allow a neutral, third party to listen to the concerns and needs of both parents to try to get both parties to agree on mutual solutions that will have the best possible outcome that is most favorable to the minor children. Take very special notice that I said *the best possible outcome that is most favorable to the minor children*, not the best possible outcome that is most favorable to you and your co-parent.

For a wide variety of reasons, mediation appointments can sometimes prove to be the most explosive moments in the divorce and child custody process. From the time that you and the other parent have legally separated, to the time that the court process begins, tempers are usually still high because both parties are usually still very angry at one another for their own individual reasons. If your mediator feels that there is still a high level of tension between you and the other parent, the mediator will recommend that each parent be interviewed separately, in an effort to prevent any unnecessary arguments or other hostile outbursts in the presence of the mediator. On the other hand, if the mediator is able to establish that both parents appear to be cordial with one another, and obviously willing to work towards solutions *together*, then the mediator will usually

---

19 Intervention between conflicting parties to promote reconciliation, settlement, or compromise.

CHAPTER 2: WHAT TO EXPECT IN COURT

be more than willing to conduct an interview with both parents present so that reasonable arrangements can be discussed, with regard to how the minor children will be taken care of.

If there could only be one suggestion that I'm able to recommend to you about showing up to your mediation appointments, it would simply be to **NOT** show up to your mediation appointment with the new person you're dating! When you show up to your scheduled mediation appointment, or any other court proceedings, with the new person that you are dating, it is a recipe for total disaster!

When you show up to court appearances with a new person that you are either dating or appear to be dating, you are sending a very strong message to the court that SCREAMS that you primarily care only about YOUR wants, YOUR needs, YOUR desires and YOUR agenda, rather than what's in the best possible interests of your children. This is not a good look! Family court is not all about you showcasing your new love interest before the court. In my opinion, this is an excellent way to position yourself to *lose* more than what you will go to court hoping to gain!

Once you have completed your interview with the court mediator, the mediator will then document the outcome of your interview so that the court will be made aware of any recommendations made by the mediator's office. The mediator's office will inform the court, in a written summary, that you and the other co-parent have either come to a mutual agreement on specific issues or if there was no agreement between the parties at all. Once this written summary of the mediator's report becomes a part of your case file, the court will review it on the date of your hearing or at your next scheduled hearing. If it becomes apparent to the court that you and your co-parent have come to a mutual agreement on the issues surrounding your case, then the court will almost always honor your agreement(s) and make it an order of the court. However, if the court reads the mediator's report and sees that you and your co-parent are consistently unable to reach mutual agreements that will be most beneficial for your children, then prepare to dish out thousands of dollars for costly attorney's fees as you go in search of an attorney to represent you.

If you truly have a desire for your legal separation, divorce or child custody process to go smoothly and be over and done with as soon as humanly possible, the only way that this can possibly happen is if you and your co-parent make a rock-solid commitment to work together during *every* phase of the legal process! The more that you and your co-parent work together, the more time and money you will both be saving. The more that you and your co-parent continue to fight it out in court, argue back and forth, bicker, refuse to cooperate with each other, refuse to obey the court's orders and continue to demonstrate childish behavior, the more money you will both spend on legal fees and court costs – you may even find yourself in jail if you refuse to change your behavior for the benefit of your children!

If you are currently experiencing any financial hardships that are adversely affecting your livelihood, and would like to embrace some extremely helpful information, then here are some modern day insights that I'm more than happy to share

CHAPTER 2: WHAT TO EXPECT IN COURT

with you.

Once you make up in your mind that you are going to be the first person (*Petitioner*) to file for divorce, prepare to spend no less than $435.00 to file your petition, if you are filing in California. Filing fees typically always vary from state to state. After you pay this initial filing fee to get your case moving forward, you will likely have to pay an additional fee to a third party to have your co-parent served. Whenever you have your co-parent served with court papers that you have filed, this process is known as **proof of service**[20].

Proof of Service simply means that you have written, documented proof that you have served the other party with a copy of the papers that you intend to show to the court at your next court hearing. Contact a few of your local law enforcement agencies to see if they have an on-duty **process server**[21] that will deliver your court documents to your co-parent. If so, they will likely charge you a small fee for this type of service. If your local law enforcement agencies do not have a process server to assist you with completing the proof of service process, then someone who works in the court clerk's office should be able to direct you to the appropriate place to get the help you need.

Typically speaking, the price for hiring a third party to complete your proof of service can range anywhere from $50.00 up to about $75.00. If those fees prove to be too much for you,

---

20 A statement submitted (as by a sheriff) to the court as evidence of successful service of process to a party.

21 A person who serves legal documents, as subpoenas, writs, or warrants, especially those requiring appearance in court.

then you can always use a close friend or family member (who is not a party to your court case) to serve your co-parent with the necessary court papers for a much lower price or possibly for free. Once your co-parent receives their copy of what you filed with the court, they will typically have anywhere between 30-45 days to file their response. When your co-parent files their response to your initial divorce filing, they will also have to pay the $435.00 fee. These filing fees mentioned above are for residents within the State of California, County of Los Angeles. Filing fees in your local court jurisdiction may vary.

For every motion that you file with the court clerk's office, there will be some type of filing fee. If you feel that you are experiencing any financial hardships, and cannot afford to pay for any court filing fees, visit the clerk's office at your local courthouse and ask them for a fee waiver application. If your fee waiver application is approved, a copy of your approved fee waiver application will stay on file with the court and you will not be charged for any eligible fees associated with any future motions that you may wish to file. Court employees are typically prohibited from offering any type of legal advice to you but, if you need any of your legal questions answered, find out if your courthouse has a Self-Help Center that can assist you with your legal matters free of charge. Filing fees for your state or court jurisdiction may vary.

If the Self-Help Center cannot successfully resolve your legal issues, the best thing for you to do is seek legal advice and/or assistance by consulting a family law attorney.

For the benefit and well-being of your child's mental and

CHAPTER 2: WHAT TO EXPECT IN COURT

emotional health, cooperate with your co-parent as often as possible so that the court can see that there is a mutual level of respect between the two of you.

Cooperating with one another throughout the court process will save you a ton of money and it will free up your valuable time to focus on more productive things. If you and your co-parent refuse to work together to raise your children in anything less than a loving, stress-free environment, then the court is going to set a trial date for the both of you so that each of you can put on evidence as to why you should get what you will likely be asking the court for.

This is an extremely risky approach to settling your divorce and child custody issues because, if you choose to go down this road, the court may very well end up making permanent orders that are not in your favor. As you will soon discover over the next few chapters, Raymond and Myra chose to do things the hard way, because they were both too stubborn to listen to sound advice to do what was in the best interest of their children. Trust me when I tell you… the court is *not* impressed with how much evidence you have against the other parent, so get that out of your mind way before you even get to court.

If you *really* want to impress the court, show up to every court appearance prepared to demonstrate to the court that you and your co-parent have already worked out your problems and have already come to an agreement on all matters concerning how you will both continue to work together to raise your children. The more things that you can agree on with your co-parent, you can basically write your own court order simply by telling the court the terms and conditions you've worked out with the other parent. Your child is counting on you to make the right choices... choose wisely!

Mental Rest Area

Based on what you've read so far, it's time to take a short mental break and reflect on the circumstances that surround your own personal separation or divorce experience. Rate yourself on how well you think you *are* handling things or how well you think you *did* handle things. Using the boxes shown below, check the box that best represents how you rate yourself (only check one box). After you rate yourself, briefly describe in your own words what you feel you could be doing better so that your child/children can best benefit from your decisions. Remember, while you are at this mental rest area, this is the time where holding yourself accountable is of the utmost importance so that your growth in this area can be accurately measured. Good, bad or indifferent, own the decisions that you've made that have not been so beneficial to your child/children, but also list the decisions that you are happy that you made – and share how those decisions were able to benefit your child/children.

- ☐ **0-4 Not Handling Things Very Well**
- ☐ **5-7 Handling Things Well**
- ☐ **8-10 Proud of How I'm Handling Things**

CHAPTER 2: WHAT TO EXPECT IN COURT

CHAPTER 3

Suck it Up!

When someone has hurt our feelings, bruised our ego, betrayed our trust, broken a promise, questioned our loyalty or even fallen out of love with us, the instinctive, human thing to do is to retaliate in some way, shape or form. As a result of many adverse circumstances, retaliating is the most common reaction that we display to show our disgust and hostile disapproval of how someone else has treated us… especially when it's a person that we've invested a significant amount of time into.

Once the word had gotten out that Raymond and Myra had officially separated and were going through a divorce, friends and family members who were once mutual supporters of the couple began to take sides. Myra's friends who once spoke so highly of Raymond were now extremely distant from him and did not like him at all. Likewise, Raymond's friends and family members who once loved Myra like their own, suddenly couldn't stand the mention of her name!

Moments like these represent the onset of both co-parents building an unnecessary team of cheerleaders who will almost always give you the worst possible ideas with regard to things you should do to get back at the other co-parent; things that are obviously **malicious**[22], but will ultimately make you feel better. This is the worst possible advice anyone could ever give you, so don't fall for it.

Shortly after Myra started to realize that her dirty deeds had come to the light, she was overwhelmed with a very somber feeling of shame and embarrassment. Even though they all stood ready to support her and her children through the divorce process, Myra's friends and family were very disappointed with her laundry list of poor choices that ultimately landed her in family court.

The more Myra felt this unbearable weight on her shoulders, she decided to channel that negative energy by making it seem like everything bad that was happening to her was Raymond's fault.

In Myra's eyes, it was Raymond's fault that she began having eyes for other men – since she felt that Raymond was not giving her enough attention. In Myra's eyes, Raymond was to blame for the fact that the court ended up making her pay child support for their son, Cameron. In Myra's eyes, it was Raymond's fault that she was left with nowhere to go once Raymond decided to move out of the home they once shared. In Myra's eyes, it

---

22 Having or showing a desire to cause harm to someone.

CHAPTER 3: SUCK IT UP!

was Raymond's fault that her reputation had been ruined by all of the alleged lies that Raymond had told about her. Are you starting to see what's missing in this scenario?

Myra was on *FIRE* about defending her name and her reputation that Raymond was so clearly trying to destroy. Taking the blame-game to its highest possible levels, Myra's irate phone calls and verbally abusive voicemail messages were just not enough to satisfy her destructive hunger for trying to make Raymond regret filing for divorce!

Myra's priorities were centered around gathering as many allies as she could so that she could appear to make Raymond look like he was the unfit co-parent. Myra felt that if she could prove to the court that Raymond was an unfit co-parent, she would end up getting sole custody of Cameron and winning a bitter custody battle against Raymond. The only problem with Myra's less than brilliant plan was that she underestimated Raymond's level of intelligence.

For every *action* there is a *reaction*. Even though Raymond knew that the only reason Myra was being vindictive and confrontational was because Raymond had left her and had publicly exposed her dirty deeds, he subsequently allowed Myra to lure him into her trap.

Approximately 30 days before Raymond moved out of the home that he once shared with Myra, he quickly took on the role of a self-appointed detective. Since Raymond had several years of military training and experience, he took it upon himself to spend countless hours investigating and tracking Myra's every move. Due to the fact that Raymond prided himself on his gifted ability to be an excellent communicator, he knew that he wanted to stick it to Myra once they got to court.

As Raymond began packing up his things, preparing to move out, he came across a multitude of random items that he felt would be useful in his divorce and child custody case. Throughout the entire duration of their relationship, Myra did not drink alcohol unless it was a very special occasion. Even during special occasions, her drinking was extremely limited and, when she did drink, she did not drink the type of alcohol that had a high percentage of alcohol.

While going through their closet, in search of any valuable items of his that he did not want to leave accessible to Myra, Raymond found a backpack hidden in the back of the closet that he had never seen in the house before. He immediately grabbed the backpack and began to comb through it to identify its contents. To his surprise, Raymond found four bottles of Vodka… all in different flavors.

One bottle had never been opened, but the other bottles were obviously consumed and were more than half empty. Raymond whipped out his camera phone and began taking pictures so that he could use them in court to convince the judge that Myra had become an alcoholic. Since that was such an impressive find for him, Raymond continued searching the closet – as if he literally had a search warrant! Next, he found a small, white box that was labeled "Crystal Dishes" on the outside. Eager to verify if the box did in fact contain crystal dishes, Raymond removed the lid from the box and had struck gold again!

CHAPTER 3: SUCK IT UP!

Inside the box was a variety of letter sized manila file folders with random papers that Myra had carefully concealed. In one of the manila file folders was a stack of bank statements from a checking account that Myra had never told Raymond about. Finding these bank statements really infuriated Raymond because, throughout the previous two years of their marriage, Myra made it a habit of always telling Raymond that she was broke whenever he asked her for money to contribute towards their household bills. Once again, Raymond took photos of particular documents so that he could prove to the court how long Myra had maintained this secret account, and what a great detective he had become. And now... for the grand finale!

In the top drawer of Myra's nightstand was a small, hardcover journal hidden underneath a stack of miscellaneous papers – a stack of papers that will have a very important message later on in this book!

As Raymond continued to flip through the pages of Myra's journal, he made a chilling discovery. He found a journal entry that was documented during a weekend that Raymond was out of town on a business trip. This journal entry went into vivid detail about *one* of the men that Myra had met at a local farmer's market while Raymond was out of town.

Not only did the journal entry describe where Myra met the mystery man, it also disclosed his full name, the city where he lived and the name of the company he worked for... all the information that a self-appointed detective like Raymond would need to strengthen his case. There's really no good reason to narrate this childish story any further because, by now, you should already be able to read between the lines to see that things in this scenario between Raymond and Myra do not get better... they absolutely get worse!

Although you may see this as a very riveting story that has unfolded between Raymond and Myra, the intended objective for telling you the story is for you to examine where YOU stand, with regards to the type of parent YOU are being in your co-parenting process.

As you were reading this chapter, did you stop to notice that not one word was said about the adverse effects that Raymond and Myra's behavior may have had on their children? Do you see *yourself* in this chapter? In your divorce or child custody matter, are YOU that parent who is more focused on trying to **crucify**[23] your co-parent for what they have seemingly done wrong that you forget to listen to the voice (needs) of your child? This very chapter is one of the primary reasons it was so important to write this book to share with parents all around the world... so that, for once, the children can win rather than the parents.

What happened between Raymond and Myra in this chapter is the very reason why children are made to feel as if *their voice* doesn't matter – when they recognize that their parents are going through a hostile divorce or custody battle. From this moment forward, I want you to understand that your child is counting on you to SUCK IT UP! Your child is counting on both parents to take care of them... to raise them in a loving

---

23 To destroy the power of.

CHAPTER 3: SUCK IT UP!

and safe environment... to nurture them when you see that a need should be addressed... to reassure them that, even though you and the other parent are parting ways, they are still very important to you.

Over the course of many, many, many years, parents have insulted the intelligence of their children by thinking that the children have no idea what is happening in the relationship between their parents. If you are the parent who has been thinking this way, today should be the last day that you continue to have this level of misguided thinking. If you continue to think along these lines, that your children are not paying attention to your destructive behaviors then, by default, your children may also find themselves duplicating these same behaviors later on in life as they transition from childhood into adulthood.

No matter how angry or disgusted you may get sometimes, because of what *you* feel that your co-parent has done wrong, you have to suck it up and be the bigger person... not for YOU, but for the benefit of your child! No matter how unfairly you may think a court has ruled against what YOU wanted to see happen at your court hearing, you have to suck it up and be the bigger parent. No matter how upset you may get after the court makes orders regarding your case that you feel are unfair, you have to suck it up and be the bigger, more responsible parent.

This is where most parents go wrong when their case is finally heard before a court of law. They go to court with such a targeted focus of making the other parent look bad, that they end up embarrassing themselves in the process! Forget about who is going to end up paying child support or not... just focus on what is going to be best for your child. Forget about how much alimony or spousal support the court might order you to pay… just focus on what is going to be best for your child. Forget about who will be granted primary physical custody *vs.* who will be granted only weekend visitations… just focus on what is going to be best for your child. Forget about the fact that your co-parent may be in a new relationship with someone else – even while your divorce has not been finalized… just focus on the things that are going to be in the best interest of your child.

I am writing this chapter in an effort to **admonish**[24] you as to how important it is that you keep 100% of your energy and focus on the needs of your child so that I can save you from the embarrassment and the heartache that I put myself through while working to bring closure to my own child custody battles. I cannot say this enough times throughout this book – the court <u>does not care</u> about what appears to be in YOUR best interest! The court only cares about what will ultimately be in the best possible interest of your child.

You are hereby being formally warned that, if you go into family court thinking that the court is going to base its orders on the fact that you personally caught your co-parent cheating on you with someone else, trust and believe me… you are going to regret it and wish you walked into court with a much different mindset! For the sake of showing the court that you are a responsible and rational parent, don't risk it! Ironically, Myra was given this same advice by her parents but, determined to handle things HER way, she didn't listen.

---

24 To give friendly, earnest advice or encouragement to.

CHAPTER 3: SUCK IT UP!

Myra was so focused on playing the victim in her child custody case, that she annoyingly involved her parents with trying to get them "on her side" whenever she would try to make Raymond appear to be the unreasonable parent. She even went as far as copying her parents on a very hateful and childish email that she sent to Raymond's job. To her surprise, Myra's parents did not take the bait. Instead, her mother responded to the email and told Myra to just humble herself, SUCK IT UP and take care of her kids.

In agreement with his wife, Myra's father had also replied to the email by telling Myra to stop worrying about what Raymond was doing and just focus on being the great mother that they felt she could be. He issued her a very stern warning to swallow her pride and put the needs of her children before her own. As you will later discover, Myra chose to ignore the advice of her parents and decided to continue doing things HER way and, in the end, she paid a very costly price for her decisions.

Raymond was not necessarily a saint throughout the divorce and child custody **shenanigans**[25] but, after a multitude of people had called him out for the things that he was not handling appropriately, he eventually started to learn his lessons from the bad things that were just starting to happen to Myra. Sometimes, as a way to stay humble and keep the lines of communication open between you and your co-parent, you are going to have to learn how to agree to disagree.

You are not always going to see eye-to-eye on things; you

---

25 Tricky or questionable practices or conduct.

are not always going to have the mental or emotional strength to even deal with your co-parent at times, but you must always put forth your best effort to agree on things that are best for your child – even when it means going out of your way or appearing to be inconvenienced. You should never look at what's best for your child as being an inconvenience. The more that you *practice* getting along with your co-parent and working together to find solutions for the best possible outcomes, the more **leniencies**[26] you may receive from the court as that need arises.

On the other hand, if you and your co-parent are constantly showing obvious signs that you can never get along to work in the best interest of your child, then it may be in your best interest to seek out a good attorney who specializes in family law matters and retain them to represent you. Trying to effectively co-parent with one another when there is hatred, bitterness, stubbornness, selfishness and egotistical decision-making is a guaranteed recipe for complete failure! Your biggest WINS are always going to come in the form of seeing the smiles of happiness on your child's face on a regular basis, even in times where there may be an occasional flare-up of misunderstandings.

If you already know that you cannot afford to pay steep legal fees or ongoing court costs for filing unnecessary motions, then it is in the best interests of both parents to get along as often as possible, and continue working together so that the court does not have to intervene. If the court has to get involved because you and the other parent refuse to get along and work together,

---

26 A disposition to show kindness or compassion.

CHAPTER 3: SUCK IT UP!

then the court has the power and the authority to make orders that will prove to be a costly wake-up call for both of you. No matter how hostile your co-parent may become with you out in public, via email or even by leaving you threatening voicemail messages, never fight with your co-parent out in a public setting. Simply document the unreasonable communication or behavior by the other parent and let the court determine how that will be handled. Never fight with your co-parent in front of your children or out in public places... fight them in court instead. Acting out of emotion in the heat of the moment can cause irreversible damage that can spill over into the lives of all parties with an interest of seeing that the children are always taken care of.

Are YOU willing to risk losing everything that you appear to be working so hard to gain, all for the sake of being defiant and not listening to good, sound advice? Choose your answer carefully... your child is counting on you to make the best decision that will benefit *them!*

Mental Rest Area

Now that you have finished learning about a new scenario, on the lines provided, describe whether you have been acting more like Raymond or more like Myra. Regardless of which person you choose, write down some things that you feel like YOU can do much better in YOUR co-parenting process than Raymond and Myra did.

THEIR VOICE MATTERS

CHAPTER 3: SUCK IT UP!

CHAPTER 4

Shaping Your Child's Future

Before you dive into this chapter, I want you to clear your thoughts and remain very open-minded to what I am about to say. Your child did not *ask* to be here on earth… YOU brought them here during the "heat of the moment!" Regardless of whether or not their conception came *after* you got married or *during* a heated, passionate episode of self-centered lust, long before marriage was even a consideration, YOU either responsibly or irresponsibly asked for them to be here.

Throughout the course of your child's life, he or she will be exposed to countless numbers of people who can and will influence their life in some form or fashion. During the most impressionable years of their development, you will play the most vital role in what *types* of people your child is or is not exposed to.

Once both parents find that they have reached their breaking point in their marriage, or alternative relationship, it becomes so easy to lose sight of the most precious things in life that they will always share between them... their children.

In this chapter, I want to compel you to think outside the box on a regular basis so that you can see your children in a way that you've never pictured them before. To get your mental gears shifting in the right direction, complete the exercise below. The only thing you will need for this exercise is a positive attitude and access to YouTube.

Exercise #1

Go to the official website for YouTube. In the YouTube search engine, type in the words: Making Pottery on the Wheel.

You will then see a wide variety of videos that will appear with demonstrations on how to make various types of objects such as: candle holders, coffee mugs, tea pots, vases or large, decorative bowls. Select three different short videos on how to make three different pottery objects and then continue reading the remainder of this chapter. Each video that you watch should be under 10 minutes in length. STOP HERE until you have watched all three videos.

The reason why you were asked to select and watch three different videos on making pottery is because each video you watched has three very important similarities. Regardless of the items that were being made in each of the three videos, you should have also been able to identify similarities in the *materials* that were needed to create the pottery items in the

CHAPTER 4: SHAPING YOUR CHILD'S FUTURE

videos. First, it took an actual *person* sitting down at the controls of the pottery wheel to shape the intended object into its desired form. Secondly, it took a nice sized *bucket* or *bowl of water* to help mold the clay with ease. Lastly, it took a healthy amount of *clay* to create and shape the intended object.

Do you remember what the person in the video looked like who was controlling the pottery wheel? I now want you to imagine that YOU are that person controlling the pottery wheel! Do you remember seeing the pottery maker continuously dipping his/her hands in a bucket or bowl of water as he/she was shaping the clay? Well, rather than thinking of it as a bowl or a bucket of water, I now want you to imagine things like: love, **empathy**[27], compassion, integrity, protection, kindness, support, encouragement, loyalty, happiness, fun, excitement, influence, quality time and sacrifice being inside of that bowl or that bucket instead of the water. Remember that healthy amount of clay that you saw placed in the center of the pottery wheel in the three videos?

I no longer want you to think of it as a ball of clay... I want you to now think of that ball of clay as your child! Now that I have positioned you to think outside the box again, this chapter is about to teach you that you are not shaping a ceramic bowl... a coffee mug or a decorative dinner plate... you are shaping an innocent life!

From the time they're born to the time they reach their late

---

27 The action of understanding, being aware of, being sensitive to, and vicariously experiencing the feelings, thoughts and experience of another.

teens, *you*, their parent, will be their absolute biggest influencer. Your choices, or your inability to make the right choices when appropriate, are symbolic to the person's hands on the ball of clay as the pottery wheel begins to spin. The actions that you take while in the presence of your child are what will ultimately mold them and shape them into the person that they are likely to become as they grow older.

If you raise your child in a happy home where there is love, peace, unity, respect, accountability, rules, structure and the expectation of setting goals and working hard, then your child stands a very good chance of duplicating the types of productive behaviors that are typically present in these kinds of environments. Under these circumstances, these character traits are similar to the water that is used by the potter to mold his/her clay into the object that is being created. On the other hand, if you raise your child in a hostile, chaotic, dysfunctional, problematic or confrontational home, then there is a high probability that your child will duplicate these counter-productive behaviors as they get older. Whatever environment you choose to raise your child in, you are molding and shaping their future by how you talk, by how you act and by how you handle conflict.

Looking at your current situation that may have landed you in family court in the first place, what do you think YOU are molding your child into becoming by how they have witnessed *you* behaving? Are you molding your child into a respectful, mild-mannered person who feels comfortable with talking to you about anything that may be bothering them? Are you molding your child into a fearful, overly-introverted or even

CHAPTER 4: SHAPING YOUR CHILD'S FUTURE

depressed person because you think that yelling, cursing, fighting or verbally abusing your co-parent in front of your child is the proper way to handle conflict? These are extremely important questions to ask yourself, because whatever answers you come up with will be evidence of how you are shaping your child's life… whether you want to own it or not!

It is imperative that you remember that, in many domestic conflicts, your child does not have a say in what happens to them as a result of how you and your co-parent communicate with each other – they don't have a voice. Since your child is a minor, and does not have a voice with regards to how *they* might wish to be taken care of and loved, this book is *their* voice! *Their Voice Matters* is an intentional reminder to you that *their* feelings matter… *their* opportunities matter… *their* mental health matters… *their* fears matter… *their* concerns matter… *their* needs matter… *their* hopes and dreams matter… their goals matter… *their* freedoms matter… *their* chance for a better future matters… *their voice* matters!

Mothers… do you want your daughters to be promiscuous as they grow from childhood into adulthood? Do you want to see your daughters disrespecting themselves by how they dress and reveal the most sacred parts of their bodies? Do you want to see your daughters in toxic relationships with boys or men who treat them like "property" instead of men who treat them like "Queens?" Do you want to see your daughters in relationships with boys or men who only want to be with them for sexual gratification? Do you want to see your innocent little daughters hooked on drugs at the most precious and impressionable stages of their lives?

If you also answered 'No' to either of these questions, then you also need to stop allowing your daughters to see YOU acting like this *if* you are displaying these types of behaviors. If you do not want to see your daughters go through life constantly attracting the kind of men who will physically, mentally and emotionally abuse them, then maybe you need to start holding yourself more accountable for the types of men that you allow your daughters to be exposed to… *if* you are exhibiting these types of behaviors!

If you are constantly allowing your daughters to see you in relationship after relationship where the man treats you terribly, what type of example are you setting for your daughters? This has been a very vicious cycle since the beginning of time, but the cycle CAN be broken if you're willing to level up and do the work it will take to get you there! If you truly desire to see your child living a very good quality of life as they learn how to find their way in this world, the training to get them to that stage doesn't start once they turn 18… it starts NOW!

Fathers… do you want your sons to beat on women when they become adults? Do you want your sons to be verbally, mentally and emotionally abusive to women when they can't always have their way? Do you want to see your sons end up in county jail or state prison for hurting others, all because they were never taught by YOU how to control their anger or their temper? Is it your desire to see your sons doing time in prison for participating in gang violence or doing drugs? If you answered 'No' to either of these questions, then you need to stop allowing

CHAPTER 4: SHAPING YOUR CHILD'S FUTURE

your sons to see YOU acting like this *if* you are displaying these types of behaviors. As an "allegedly" mature parent, you should already know by now that kids are like sponges; they are going to soak in all of the things that they see you do and hear you say. When your sons witness you out in public acting like a fool when you can't get your way then, as *they* grow up, what you're actually doing is teaching them that acting like a fool is the appropriate way to behave when someone doesn't give them what they want. Only a parent striving for failure would allow themselves to behave this way.

Parents... the things that your children say or do while they are out in the eye of the public, good, bad or downright horrific, is a direct reflection of how *you* are raising them at home! It is also a reflection of the types of environments and people that you may be consistently subjecting them to. Your home should be their primary training grounds for the life-lessons that they will need to eventually learn to be productive and thriving members of our society.

Although they have the ability to learn a wide variety of skills or trades while they are in school, it is not their *teacher's* responsibility to raise them up in the way that they should go... that is YOUR responsibility. Even when you have raised your children with great values, morals and the ethical principles of having integrity in all that they do, they may still go astray and make poor choices and decisions that are not conducive to how you raised them. Use those moments as training opportunities to teach them how they can make a better choice the next time they are confronted with conflict. If you feel like there may be a possibility that you have not been doing such a good job with raising your child to be the best possible version of themselves that they can be, LET TODAY BE A NEW DAY for you to forgive yourself and move forward with a fresh, new start.

Rather than letting your ego and your stubbornness get the best of you, put these useful tips to good use for the sake and benefit of your child. Raising children takes the willful participation of both parents. Just as Myra's parents had tried to warn her on numerous occasions, swallow your pride when conflict arises and always make choices and decisions that are in the best interest of your child. When all is said and done, you'll be glad that you did!

Mental Rest Area

On the lines below, write down some key takeaways that you got from reading this chapter. After reading this chapter, do you think your actions are setting your child up to have a *productive* future or a *counter-productive* future? What mistakes have you made as a parent that you will now commit to working harder at in dealing with your co-parent? Your growth as a parent will depend heavily on how honest you are with yourself in answering these questions.

_____
_____
_____
_____

CHAPTER 4: SHAPING YOUR CHILD'S FUTURE

CHAPTER 5

Choose Your Advisors Carefully

For parents and co-parents that find themselves headed to family court for either legal separation, divorce or child custody matters for the very first time, anxiety levels can easily become very high because neither parent is fully aware of what to expect once they get to court. By the time your friends, family members and even co-workers find out that you will soon be going through a child custody battle in family court, you will soon see for yourself that there will be no shortage of people who will want to offer you advice as to how you should handle yourself throughout *your* legal proceedings. There are always pros and cons to consider when trying to decide if you are being offered helpful advice or if you are being offered terrible advice… so choose your advisors carefully!

When taking into consideration what advice to take from others, versus what advice to ignore, get into the habit of asking yourself the right types of questions so that you can either validate or disqualify the information you are being offered. Do you trust the person giving you advice, knowing that you could lose your parental rights if they give you bad information? Has the person offering you advice had a successful, long-term relationship that you respect and look up to? Does the person you are taking advice from have a proven history of making the right decisions? Is the person you are taking advice from a productive contributor to society? Does the person you are taking advice from love your child more than you do? Does the person you are taking advice from have a reputation for being in one toxic relationship after another?

    The reason why these are all important questions to ask yourself is because, if you buy someone else's opinion… you also buy their lifestyle! If the person that you are constantly taking advice from has a history or reputation for making poor decisions, then you are likely to make those poor decisions as well if you decide to take their advice. DO NOT take counter-productive advice, simply to show your allegiance or your loyalty to the person who gave you the information – just because you've known them for a long time. If the person that you are taking advice from has a long-standing history of making proper and wise decisions, then their recommendations to you regarding certain family law matters may prove to be very beneficial to you *and* your child.

    No matter who you choose to take advice from, at the end of the day, the ultimate decisions that will have to be made will

CHAPTER 5: CHOOSE YOUR ADVISORS CAREFULLY

have to be made by you. Rather than learning the hard way, by doing only what is in YOUR best interests, let Myra's behaviors in the previous chapter teach you some valuable and priceless lessons that you can build from on your journey to becoming a better parent.

Because they are typically eager to prove their allegiance towards your friendship, best friends (BFF's) are some of the most dangerous people to take legal advice from! While I have your attention, I'd like to introduce you to Myra's best friend, "Miranda."

Miranda and Myra have known each other ever since the 3rd grade, and have been besties from 5th grade all the way into their adulthood. Over the course of many years, they have supported each other through thick and thin. Just so that you understand a little bit about Miranda's background, here are some distinct characteristics to remember.

She is only 33 years old with four small children by three different men. She has never been married and dropped out of college during the third semester of her first year. In her lifetime, Miranda has served time in jail on two separate occasions – once for possession of a controlled substance and once for check fraud. Based on **substantiated**[28] allegations by the father of one of her children, Miranda lost custody of ALL of her children for approximately six months. During this period of time, all of the children were placed in the custody of their respective grandparents. Miranda's history of making consistently bad

---

28 To establish by proof or competent evidence; to verify.

choices and poor decisions ultimately led to the laundry list of hardships that she was forced to endure; she was a victim of her own actions. The moment that Miranda found out that Raymond had filed for divorce from Myra, it was all downhill from there for Myra! Since Raymond was a more distinctively responsible parent than Myra, Miranda knew that Myra would have an uphill custody battle, and she was willing to help "Myra" win under any circumstances!

When Miranda found out that the court had ordered Myra to pay child support to Raymond, she became so upset that she immediately began advising Myra on what papers to file with the court to get her child support payments reduced so that *Myra* could pocket more money. As if this wasn't already enough to direct Myra's attention away from helping Raymond to support their child, Miranda invites Myra to a house party with the intent to introduce her to a male friend that she feels Myra would be the perfect match for.

Predictably, Myra takes the bait and agrees to go to the house party. She finally met the man that Miranda was trying to set her up with, and the rest was history! In the weeks and months following this party, Myra spent the majority of her free time developing her relationship with her new love interest, rather than trying to develop a better relationship between her and her children. Please keep in mind that, while Myra is now involved in this new relationship with a man that she's barely known for 60 days, her divorce is nowhere close to being finalized.

As the plot continues to thicken, Miranda urges Myra to get revenge against Raymond and take him for all he's got! Once

CHAPTER 5: CHOOSE YOUR ADVISORS CAREFULLY

again, Myra, all wrapped up in her feelings, takes the bait. Even if the chaos does not *exactly* fit your current situation, do you see how much negative energy is being spent on unnecessary drama, rather than all parties involved staying in solution mode? Now do you see how easy it is for the voice of your child to be drowned out by the sounds and actions of relentless bickering between selfish and childish adults? Now do you see why *their voice matters*?

From this moment forward, Myra's only concern was thinking of ways that she could work against Raymond in the child custody proceedings, rather than work *with* him for the sake of their son, Cameron. Though it seemed like a good idea in the beginning, at least in *her* mind, Myra's choice to continue going down this road was only evidence that she would ultimately be losing everything that she thought she was going to gain. Raymond was also no angel in the very beginning… he also made his share of regretful mistakes.

Being the alpha male that he was, Raymond's conscience would not let him forget that other men had come into the picture and compromised his relationship with Myra – the love of his life. The more he thought about it, the more he created a false sense of justification within his own mind to react to every horrible thing that he felt that Myra had done. This went on between Myra and Raymond for so long that, by the time their divorce was officially finalized, the judge had already retired!

Initially, Raymond was following Myra around – trying to see who she was dating, where she was going, what she was doing and who she was doing it with. The more that Raymond's friends and family saw him conducting himself in this way, they would always pull him aside and point out to him how silly he was being by doing these kinds of things that were completely out of character for him. They often told him that the amount of time he was spending trying to gather information about things that no longer mattered, could have been quality time spent with his child instead.

It didn't take long for Raymond to figure out that the malicious things that Myra was trying to do to him were only being done because she was taking advice from all of the wrong types of people who no longer liked him. He also figured out that, the more malicious Myra got with her antics, the more things continued to spiral out of control for her in court… and he decided that he wanted no parts of the court's wrath!

The difference between Myra and Raymond was that, over time, Raymond was finally following the advice of multiple people in his circle that loved him enough to give him valid, helpful advice that would benefit his son, Cameron. By default, Raymond would also have access to these benefits and resources he needed to responsibly provide for Cameron. Myra, on the other hand, was still allowing her pride to get the best of her and she quickly developed a reputation with the court that did not cast a positive light on her.

It took Raymond a long time to get it together but, the more he found himself focusing on his child and what was best for him, all of the things that he was fighting for in court started to fall into place. When the court began to grant Raymond's requests on a more frequent basis, he immediately began to

CHAPTER 5: CHOOSE YOUR ADVISORS CAREFULLY

notice that staying focused on what was in the best interest of his child was allowing him to see the types of results that he wanted to see, from a legal perspective as well as from a parental perspective. Raymond was always able to provide his child with a regimented, supportive and stable environment. He did not want anything to stand between him being able to continue that on a long-term basis. Rather than making a reckless decision to continue behaving like Myra, Raymond demonstrated his love and **adoration**[29] for his son by taking advantage of the helpful information that was being given to him by people who wanted to see him succeed in his endeavors.

If someone you know claims to be a true friend of yours, yet they are continuously giving you horrific advice as to how you should be handling legal matters that have the ability to adversely affect how often the court will allow you to see your child, you should STOP taking advice from that person IMMEDIATELY! A person that gives you toxic advice, and disguises that same advice as a solution to fix your problems, is only making matters more difficult for you… not better! When people say that they're your friend, but they give you the same type of advice that they would give an enemy, it is your sole responsibility to begin questioning the integrity of that friendship and strongly consider stepping far away from it.

No matter how you may look at it, a person who sincerely wants to see you and your child win and thrive, is not going to give you counter-productive advice that will cause you to

---

29 The act of adoring; the state of being adored.

lose everything that you are fighting for. In this day and age, it is very apparent that common sense is not always so common. For the sake of your child having both parents actively involved in his/her life to help guide them toward a successful future, you MUST be very careful who you choose to take advice from.

If you are the type of parent that cares more about showing allegiance to a friend, instead of showing allegiance to your child, then your irresponsible actions will be all that a court of law needs to see a pattern of inappropriate behaviors that are not in any way favorable to your child. The courts will always be more concerned with the things that you *do* rather than the things you *say*; actions speak way louder than words. If you have a "Miranda" somewhere in your life, do not go to that person for advice of any kind if you desire to see a successful outcome to your child custody or family law matters.

Should you ever have the need to go to your closest friends or family members for their advice, they are not always going to tell you what you *want* to hear! If your friends and family members love you as much as they may say they do, they are going to tell you what you *need* to hear, even if they know that you are going to be defensive once they say it. Sometimes when a person loves you, you have to know that they love you enough to tell you that you're handling a situation the wrong way, and that your actions are not in the best interest of your child. You're not always going to want to hear that from people but, if the love you have for your child is deep enough, you ought to be embracing those people in your life that are going to tell you what is right.

CHAPTER 5: CHOOSE YOUR ADVISORS CAREFULLY

Even when you feel as though you have argued your most important points in court, the court is not always going to rule in your favor. If you walk into court thinking that the court is going to rule in your favor just because you are wearing a brand new suit, you are in for a rude awakening! If you walk into court thinking that the court is going to rule in your favor just because you have on a tight mini-skirt and showing a little bit of cleavage, you are also in for a rude awakening. If you walk into court thinking that the court is going to rule in your favor just because you're sitting next to your paid attorney that drives an $85,000.00 car, then you are still in for a very rude awakening.

When people find out that you are going through a divorce or child custody battle, they are always going to be eager to give you *their* opinion about what *they* think you should do and *how* you should go about doing it. They will oftentimes share with you all of the things that helped *them* bring their divorce or child custody matters to a close, but just because a situation worked out for *them* in a particular way, it does not mean that things will work out that way for YOU! Every divorce or child custody case is very special in nature and the outcomes are going to vary, based on a wide variety of circumstances that are sometimes going to be beyond your control… so get mentally prepared for it.

Don't get yourself caught up in showing so much allegiance to friends or family members who may want to offer you information that is not so helpful, rather than showing your allegiance to your child who needs your allegiance more than anyone else on the planet! As you identify the people in your circle who are always giving you advice, and you begin to see a pattern of things constantly falling apart all around you after taking their advice, that is the moment when you need to stop and realize that you are getting the wrong information… from the wrong people… for the wrong reasons. If this is you, it's time to start doing something different so that you can start seeing some different results. If you continue to do what you've always done, you're going to keep on getting what you've always gotten.

It is always better for you and your situation if you start to develop the habit of seeking advice from people who already have a proven track record of wanting to see you WIN rather than see you get knocked down by more adversity when you may already be at a low point in your life. You may not see the value in what I'm saying at this moment because you may not have started your legal proceedings yet but, take my word for it, you do not want to go into court with a hostile tone of voice or with a confrontational attitude because, if you do, you will absolutely regret it before all is said and done.

Mental Rest Area

On the lines below, write down which character(s) in this chapter best describes how you have been carrying yourself in your child custody/divorce matter. Have you been acting more like Myra or have you been acting more like Raymond? With the above scenario in mind, what things can you be doing better to place your child in the best position to win? Be careful *and*

CHAPTER 5: CHOOSE YOUR ADVISORS CAREFULLY

intentional in how you answer these questions, because your actions must fit the type of response that you give. Do not try to persuade yourself to believe that you have been handling all of your responsibilities maturely and properly if you know there are some things that you can be doing better for the benefit of your child. Honesty wins!

CHAPTER 6

Setting Traps for the Other Parent

As mentioned by best-selling author, Yehuda Berg, "*Hurt people hurt people. That's how pain patterns gets passed on, generation after generation.*" Although the quote has been repeated by a wide variety of people, the phrase continues to receive national attention. This very quote is constantly being used by a vast number of professional organizations and companies that specialize in helping their clients heal from conditions such as: childhood trauma, domestic violence, post-traumatic stress disorder (PTSD) and other mental health disorders that are centered around physical, emotional or psychological abuse or trauma.

Imagine the stress and the fear of being at the scene of an active shooter incident. Imagine that moment where there is complete and utter chaos. There is an overwhelming sense of terror and mass confusion as people scatter to take cover to protect themselves against an enemy they most likely cannot even see. Now, try to imagine not knowing the direction of where the shots are coming from, yet simultaneously realizing that there is nowhere to run and nowhere to hide from the gunfire! Would you agree that this is a scenario where a great deal of vulnerability exists? Would you further agree that, in this type of a moment, the shooter had more than just one unfair advantage over unsuspecting victims?

When your co-parent has the right amount of knowledge about your vulnerabilities or weaknesses, this kind of knowledge can prove to be one of the biggest and most effective resources to be used against you. Always remember that the people who have known you for the longest period of time know the most about you. Therefore, they know what makes you angry; they know what makes you sad; they know what makes you happy; they know if you're good at holding grudges; they know if you're honest; they know if you are unforgiving and malicious; they know if you are weak-minded; they know if you are strong-willed; they know if you are highly intelligent; they know if you are naïve; they know if you are either responsible or irresponsible; they know if you are educated or uneducated and they know exactly what buttons to push to set you off and make you lash out to the point of hostile aggression.

The people who know the most about you also know exactly what to do to provoke you into reacting in a way that you would not ordinarily react, simply because you allowed them to make you angry. Allowing someone to have *this* much power and control over your emotions can have a devastating effect on your quality of life.

There may one day come a time that you are going to be tempted to try your absolute best to provoke your co-parent into doing something that you feel the court is going to punish them for at a future court hearing. There may one day come a time when you may feel **compelled**[30] to call the police on your co-parent, hoping to get them arrested just so that you can get a copy of the police report to take to family court and argue that your co-parent is unfit to care for your child. To give you a better idea of how these behaviors can adversely affect your pending divorce or child custody case, you are about to learn some extremely valuable lessons at the expense of Raymond and Myra.

Reporting Child Abuse or Neglect

In many child custody cases, child abuse and/or neglect are typically not reported because the child is in danger, they are reported because one parent is angry at the other parent. Oftentimes the parent who is awarded either primary physical custody or sole custody, feels like they are in a position of *"control"* just because they have the highest percentage of custody or parenting time. Not the case! In fact, as you will see in forthcoming chapters, it is that very type of attitude that will cause a parent to end up with very limited or no custody at all.

---

30 To cause to do or occur by overwhelming pressure.

In Raymond and Myra's case, Raymond **sporadically**[31] struggled with the fact that Myra had been unfaithful during their marriage and was seeing a variety of different men. Since he was awarded primary physical custody of their son, Cameron, Raymond took it upon himself to use those benefits to control Myra. Even though she was hammered with personal questions from him on a regular basis, Myra made it clear to Raymond that he didn't need to know what was going on in her house. Raymond, on the other hand, felt that he needed to know everything that was going in Myra's house, based on the fact that Cameron would spend all weekends and every other major holiday with Myra.

If Cameron came back home to Raymond with one suspicious cut, bruise, scratch or other physical alteration, Raymond immediately interrogated Myra about how the injury occurred. If Myra refused to answer his questions, or gave him a less than logical explanation, Raymond was determined to get to the bottom of it by forcing Myra to provide him with a valid reason… all by placing a simple phone call.

Focused and determined to retaliate, Raymond would often place repeated phone calls to Child Protective Services (CPS) to report Cameron's suspicious injuries as neglect or abuse by Myra. Equally focused and determined to retaliate, it wasn't long before Myra seized *her* opportunity to do the same to Raymond. This back and forth display of childish behavior went on between Raymond and Myra for more than three years.

---

31 In a sporadic manner; not regularly or constantly.

CHAPTER 6: SETTING TRAPS FOR THE OTHER PARENT

This is how children become psychologically and emotionally damaged well into their adult lives. Myra and Raymond were so focused on retaliating against each other, neither one of them took the time out to even consider how their dysfunctional actions and behaviors were continuing to make their children feel like their voice didn't matter. Does this chapter sound like anything close to what you've been experiencing? If this is starting to sound like how you have been behaving, hopefully you are already starting to identify a few ways that you can start improving your behaviors for the benefit of your child.

In this scenario, both Raymond and Myra had been advised on numerous occasions that neither one of their reports to CPS resulted in adverse actions by the agency – all of their reports were closed as being either **inconclusive**[32] or **unfounded**[33] because the agency never found evidence of abuse or neglect. Due to the fact that CPS *was* able to establish a pattern of false reporting by both Raymond *and* Myra, each of them were given a written warning by the agency that, if they received anymore false reports against each other that resulted in inconclusive or unfounded findings, the parent initiating the false report would be fined $500.00.

If you are the co-parent that desires to save as much money as you possibly can, because you are already facing financial hardships in other areas of your life, do not be the co-parent that is found to be in violation of making continuous, false

---

32 Leading to no conclusion or definite result.
33 Lacking a sound basis; groundless, unwarranted.

reports against the other co-parent simply because you want to be in control of what you have no business being in control of. Let this be a valuable lesson for you to keep your focus on the physical health, mental health and overall well-being of your child.

In an effort to discourage you from making false or otherwise unnecessary reports against your co-parent, let this online publication by *childwelfare.gov* be your inspiration to handle conflict more appropriately. The article makes it crystal clear by stating, "Upon conviction, the reporter can face jail terms ranging from 90 days to 5 years or fines ranging from $500 to $5,000. Florida imposes the most severe penalties: In addition to a court sentence of 5 years and $5,000, the Department of Children and Family Services may fine the reporter up to $10,000."

Drama in the Workplace

By this time, Myra has suffered her share of embarrassments and defeats. Following the less than helpful advice of random family members and so-called friends, Myra continues to dig holes for herself in ways that vividly demonstrate that she is truly a woman scorned.

For several weeks straight, Myra had been trying to contact Raymond by phone. Her reasoning for reaching out to him was to ask him if he would be willing to allow their son, Cameron, to stay with her for the entire week of her birthday. A few of Myra's family members were planning to fly in from out of

CHAPTER 6: SETTING TRAPS FOR THE OTHER PARENT

state to spend time with her for her birthday, and they also wanted to meet Cameron for the first time while they were in town. Not only did Raymond not ever answer his phone when Myra tried to call him, he also never returned her phone calls, based on all of the voicemail messages she left him. Raymond's refusal to return her calls or make himself available to her for discussion, infuriated Myra. By no means was this a very constructive idea, but Myra took it upon herself to take a little drive up to Raymond's job with the intent to cause a horrific scene that would hopefully get Raymond fired, in retaliation for Raymond ignoring her.

Just as she had methodically planned it, Myra finally made it to Raymond's office and, once she found him, she caused a scene that nearly got *her* arrested. Explaining to her that his office was neither the time nor the place for them to be publicly discussing their child custody issues, Raymond urged Myra to leave his job and stop causing a scene. Refusing to comply with his wishes, Myra continued shouting profanities and threats towards Raymond, and Raymond's supervisor ultimately called the police to have Myra removed from the premises.

Once Raymond obtained a copy of the police report that documented Myra's public disturbance at his job, he supplied the court a copy of the police report at their next court hearing so that the court could be made aware of Myra's absurd behavior while at Raymond's place of employment.

I want you to understand the magnitude of why this type of behavior makes you look like a terrible parent. Your child is dependent on you *and* your co-parent to provide for them. Each parent must make an honest living to provide food, clothing and shelter for their child. If you are *not* the parent with primary physical custody, yet you are always making relentless efforts to cause the other co-parent to lose their job, what you are actually doing is increasing your child's chances of having less food to eat and possibly be two steps closer to being homeless if the primary caregiver loses his/her job because of *your* actions.

The parent who has primary physical custody was awarded that level of custody by the court for a reason. The court obviously felt that the parent with primary physical custody was the best parent that would be responsible enough to continue providing a stable living environment for the child but, because you want to continue feeding your ego and your passion for thinking only about yourself, you are trying to jeopardize the livelihood of your child by trying to get your co-parent fired. How much sense does that make? Let me help you out... NONE! If you are the co-parent who has been doing this, you are demonstrating that you do not love your child and that you do not want the best for them.

This type of behavior is exactly why *their voice matters*! It is this type of unhealthy behavior that proves my point that children have no voice when it comes to the fact that their parents oftentimes practice third grade communication tactics that are counter-productive to the growth, development and mental health of their child. When parents conduct themselves in this manner, whether inside or outside of their child's presence, it insults the intelligence of the child by assuming that they are not smart enough to know what's going on between the two

CHAPTER 6: SETTING TRAPS FOR THE OTHER PARENT

parents.

This is why *Their Voice Matters* is the voice of children all around the globe who are the real victims of feuding parents who have seemingly lost their ability to make rational decisions that demonstrate their love for their children. When all you think about on a daily basis is setting traps for your co-parent to get caught up in, all you are really doing, hypothetically speaking, is wrapping more and more rope around your own neck! If you think about the most innovative and malicious ways to get your co-parent in trouble with the court, more than you think about ways to be a better parent to your child, you are already setting yourself up for total failure.

Once upon a time in my own life, while fighting my own divorce and child custody battles, I have personally witnessed endless episodes of bickering, fighting, complaining, belittling, hateful, verbally abusive and confrontational behaviors of other parents unfold in the courtroom right before my very eyes. Explaining it to you is one thing, but witnessing these things in court with your own eyes and ears is unlike anything you will ever experience in your life! The moment I heard each parent open up their mouth to have their cases heard, it was painfully obvious to see how much each parent hated each other.

The parents were so angry and hateful towards one another, all I could do is sit there and wonder, "Do these people even remember that they have a child together that needs their undivided attention in raising them?"

As mentioned in previous chapters, I remind you that this is NOT the type of mindset that parents and their co-parent want to have when they go before the court to address their unresolved issues. My co-parent and I were among many parents who had to learn the significance of these lessons the hard way. Once the court saw that we were making no effort to get along for the mutual benefit of our children, the court made orders in our family law case that made life extremely difficult and uncomfortable for the both of us, but humbling nevertheless.

It was during these moments of humility that I began to understand and accept the level of authority and power that the court had over our case. In my opinion, this is a big reason why many parents and co-parents also find that they have to learn things the hard way – because these particular parents have spent so many years of their lives being rebellious against authority and failing to accept that laws are in place for a very important reason – to maintain order and preserve the right to **due process**[34] as a means to settle matters fairly and impartially.

If you are curious to know what happened to Myra after Raymond reported the confrontational incident that took place at his job, the court gave Myra some life-changing options. The court advised Myra that she could either act like a mature adult, or she could spend 15 days in jail if she were to ever go up to Raymond's job to cause problems again or make another false report to CPS against Raymond. Which would YOU choose?

---

34 A course of formal proceedings (such as legal proceedings) carried out regularly and in accordance with established rules and principles.

CHAPTER 6: SETTING TRAPS FOR THE OTHER PARENT

Mental Rest Area

In this section, write down some additional reasons why you think that it was out of line for Myra to have gone up to Raymond's place of business to confront him. Also, write down a few ideas about how Myra could have handled that situation more effectively and more responsibly.

_____
_____
_____
_____
_____
_____
_____
_____
_____
_____
_____
_____
_____
_____
_____
_____
_____
_____

CHAPTER 7

Understanding Their Language

Now that you have made it this far in your reading, I'm sure that there are a flood of scenarios and situations that have been replaying over and over in your mind. I hope that the drama between Raymond and Myra has opened up your eyes to see some areas in your own life where you need to make some immediate changes, so that the quality of life for your child doesn't ever have to be compromised.

If you truly love your child and want to see them have the best possible life, this chapter will challenge your love. If you truly desire for your child to have a much better childhood than the childhood that you had, this chapter will challenge that desire. By the time you reach the end of this chapter, you will have definitive results as to if your behaviors throughout your child custody process are going to be all about YOU or is it going to be all about YOUR CHILD.

THEIR VOICE MATTERS

Now that you have hopefully decided to stand on your commitment of wanting to see your child have the best possible life and have a much better childhood than the one you had, this will most likely be the hardest chapter in this book for you to read. No matter how many times this chapter becomes an emotional trigger-point for you, do the right thing and take this moment to humble yourself and learn the various ways that your child speaks to you when there are really no real words for them to **utter**.[35]

No matter how many times you need to read this chapter, you need to understand that the lessons that you learn here can very well be the difference between the court granting you more time to spend with your children... or losing custody of your children until they reach the age of 18 years old.

"Daddy, please stop hitting mommy!"

"Mommy, please stop yelling at daddy!"

"Daddy, I don't like it when you are drunk all the time."

"Mommy, do we have to live here with daddy?"

"Daddy, will you please not do drugs anymore?"

"Mommy, are you ever going to come visit me and spend time with me?"

---

35 To give public expression to; express in words.

CHAPTER 7: UNDERSTANDING THEIR LANGUAGE

"Daddy, I don't want to come visit you in jail anymore. I am scared to go back to that place!"

"Mommy... I'm scared! I don't want to live here anymore!"

"When are you guys ever going to grow up?"

"Stop it... just STOP IT!!"

If your child's voice mattered to you, do you think that your child would even have the inner-confidence to ask you *any* of these questions or make *any* of these statements? Although many children do not have a high enough level of intellectual capabilities, they are expert communicators who use their body language and their behaviors to say what they cannot put into actual words.

In my experience, the most impressionable years of a child's life are between the ages of 5 to 7 years old.

These are the stages of their development in which you have to be extremely careful about what you allow them to see and hear.

All too often, adults continue to insult the intelligence of their children by assuming that they are much too young to understand the fact that mommy and daddy are always arguing and being confrontational with one another. They are not intellectually mature enough to be able to verbally articulate their displeasure of the arguing, so they act out their displeasure as their way of demonstrating how they feel about the adult behaviors that they are experiencing around them.

Because of these factors, you need to be aware that, every time you allow your child to witness a verbal, physical or emotional attack against your co-parent, you are teaching your child how to become that same angry, hateful and confrontational individual.

You must remember that, even if your co-parent did something or said something that made you extremely angry, you are lashing out against a parent that your child loves and cares about. When you become the dominant voice in an argument or physical altercation with your co-parent, in front of your child, your child becomes afraid that something horrific is about to happen to the other parent. That fear is magnified once the child internalizes the fact that, since they are only a child and have to depend on both parents for their survival, they are not strong enough to defeat the hostile parent in an effort to protect the parent that they are afraid for.

This causes a great deal of stress, anxiety and fear within your child because it makes them feel helpless and confused. If you have a child who is old enough to understand that there is obvious conflict between you and your co-parent, your constant bickering might even make your older child feel pressured into deciding which parent they love the most. Nothing good can come out of this type of dysfunctional communication.

If by chance you do have children that are old enough to understand that you and your co-parent are preparing to separate or divorce, I highly recommend that you sit your children down and explain to them that you and your co-parent have *agreed* that going your separate ways is what is best for *them* at this time. If you explain it to them in a tactful and cautious manner, you can put their mind at ease a lot faster and also decrease their stress or anxiety levels. Once your child fully understands that you and your co-parent have *agreed* on something, it suggests to your child that everything is going to be okay because mommy and daddy *agreed* to it. Even if that's a false reality, it gives your child the reassurance that you and your co-parent do not hate each other, therefore making it much easier for your child NOT to feel like they have to take one parent's side over the other during the divorce or child custody process.

I am not suggesting that you sit your kids down and discuss *every* aspect of why you and your co-parent are separating, but I am suggesting that you educate them about some very basic reasons as to why parents often split up. I am strongly recommending that you absolutely sit your children down and explain to them that the reason why you and your co-parent are splitting up is NOT their fault or because of them. This is something you *must* engrave in their minds month after month… year after year – until they are old enough to understand that you and your co-parent splitting up was probably the best thing for them for a wide variety of reasons.

All too often, children can take it upon themselves to assume that the reason why their parents are splitting up is because of them. When you are a child who is never taught or groomed to learn the dynamics of each person's role in the family unit or household, the child has no real way to make sense of the ongoing conflict in the home, because neither parent has ever practiced conflict resolution tactics on a consistent enough basis. If you and your co-parent cannot learn how to solve problems via conflict resolution methods, how do either one of you expect your child to make sense of deciding what is productive communication versus what is counter-productive communication?

"Maybe if I wasn't alive, my parents would be happier together."

"I wish I was never born!!"

"Why do my parents treat my brothers and sisters better than they treat me?"

"How come my mother never calls me or comes to visit me?"

"Why does my daddy never buy me anything for Christmas?"

"What if my parents really don't love me?"

"Why do my parents always yell at me when they are mad at each other?"

"Why do I get blamed for everything?"

CHAPTER 7: UNDERSTANDING THEIR LANGUAGE

"Why don't my parents ever tell me that they're proud of me? Am I a failure?"

"Why do the other kids in my classroom make fun of my clothes all the time?"

"Why does my mommy go to parties with her friends all the time instead of spend time with me?"

"What did I do wrong to make my parents get a divorce?"

"If mommy and daddy get a divorce, will I still have a place to live?"

If you ever heard about your child making any of the above statements to someone, how would that make you feel? If your child ever made any of these statements, would *you* be to blame for even silently empowering them to ask these questions in the first place?

I'm almost positive that, as soon as I asked you that question, your mind immediately began to try focusing on how much blame to put on your co-parent. This is an accountability question, so I'm not concerned with the blame that you desire to put on your co-parent, I'm concerned with how much accountability YOU will accept for your own actions!

These troublesome statements are how your child tries to emotionally evaluate information so that their subconscious can tell them how to feel. The reason they get comfortable with listening to their subconscious for emotional instructions, is because they do not get any verbal reassurance from their parents that everything's going to be just fine.

When I was a kid growing up, children were *seen*... not *heard*! Back in the days, children in my culture were constantly told, "Stay out of grown folks' business!" Another famous phrase was, "Mind your own business!" Merely *making* these statements was not the sole problem – the problem was HOW the statements were made!

The grown-up's tone of voice is what carried the lasting effects of making the child feel unimportant. Once you say something like that to a child, in an extremely harsh tone of voice, the child becomes fearful of engaging you in future conversations when others are around, because their subconscious warns them not to upset you again by getting involved in what may appear to be *grown folks' business*. In today's society, many of us stand in agreement that it's not WHAT you say to a person that matters... it's HOW you say it that counts.

In considering all of the information in this chapter that has led you to this point, I want to give you some examples of how your child speaks to you when they are scared, sad, depressed or just seeking your attention.

The languages that your child uses to speak to you are:

- Wetting the bed
- Unexplainable increase or decrease in appetite

CHAPTER 7: UNDERSTANDING THEIR LANGUAGE

- Sudden episodes of wanting to be withdrawn from others
- Sudden episodes of unexplainable sadness or crying
- Consistently grinding their teeth while sleeping
- Unexplainable stomach aches
- Nightmares or bad dreams
- Sudden fear of the dark
- Feeling like everything is their fault
- Sudden changes in sleeping habits
- Difficulty staying on task in school
- Constantly getting into trouble at school
- Sudden display of anger and hostility towards other students or peers
- Feeling the need to bully other children
- "Potty-Mouth Syndrome"

Of all the languages listed above, *"feeling like everything is their fault"* and *"constantly getting into trouble at school"* are the two body languages that resonate with me the most. Going back to when I was just a child, all of about six or seven years old, I witnessed a very bad divorce between my biological parents. There was endless arguing and disagreements in the home. There were also happy moments that I faintly remember but, for the most part, the arguments are what I recall the most.

Over a prolonged period of time, the consistent arguments eventually began to take a toll on me and make me feel like every adverse challenge that my parents were going through at that time was my fault. Looking back, I firmly believe that the reason I had begun to feel like everything was my fault was because neither of my parents had ever told me otherwise. Either I was told to mind my own business, or I was told nothing at all. In either event, I think I would have had a much better understanding of divorce if it were explained to me. For this reason, I have always reminded my own children that the reason I am no longer with their mother has nothing whatsoever to do with them. I always remind them that the separation was my way of providing a much better life for them, while protecting them from situations that could have hurt them.

When a child is old enough to assume that the adversities you are going through with your co-parent are *their* fault, you cannot blame them for thinking that way if you and your co-parent have never explained to them why the separation was necessary in the first place. If you leave your child to form his/her own opinions about the nature of your separation, then *their* opinion (in *their* minds) becomes factual, not because it is indeed factual, but because they have no other factors in which to measure their conclusions that either prove or disprove their perception of what's going on and why it's happening.

I was also the poster-child for getting in trouble in school on a regular basis. I was in trouble so frequently that you would have thought getting into trouble was an actual religion! As the

CHAPTER 7: UNDERSTANDING THEIR LANGUAGE

temperature in my parent's divorce began to heat up, so did my episodes of being **incorrigible**.[36]

Knowing what I know now, I was always getting into trouble because that was the safest way for me to display my disproval of how my parents were handling their divorce and custody issues. Since I knew I could never openly address my concerns to them directly, I simply acted it out in school. Since I was never asked how their problems made *me* feel, it made me a bitter and angry person at such a young age. As I got older, well into my adult years, I began to look back at my childhood to reflect on if I did something wrong. I often wondered why neither of my parents had ever sat me down to tell me that their divorce wasn't my fault. I know that feeling of self-inflicted guilt all too well. Since I could always recall how the long-term sting of divorce made ME feel as a child, I never allowed my own children to take on the guilt and emotional anguish of feeling responsible for my decision to file for divorce.

My anger was the tool I used to feel like I was punishing my parents for not wanting to hear my voice in the midst of their differences. My anger was my way of retaliating against them for not giving me a chance to be heard. I urge you *not* to put your children through what I had to go through as a child, in that regard. If you truly love your child and want to see them become a more productive member in our society, you MUST continuously remind them that their voice matters! You must

---

36 (of a person or their tendencies) not able to be corrected, improved, or reformed.

continue to remind your children that you care about how they're feeling about the life-changing issues you are trying to navigate through yourself.

You must continue to make your children feel *included* in the process. They do not have to be fully included on all levels, but give them some sense of inclusion as they get older and are able to handle the information that you share with them. If you are the parent who has been doing this, STOP talking bad about your co-parent in the presence of your child. If you continue doing that for a long enough period of time, YOU may be the parent that your child ends up hating when they become an adult and discover the truth for themselves. Don't risk losing out on a healthy, meaningful relationship with your child all because you want to bash your co-parent in their presence. You will surely regret it!

Parents who are super angry with one another always seem to want to discreetly bash the other parent in front of the child so that they can convince their child that the other co-parent is the bad guy. If you just focus on being the parent that your child is counting on you to be, as your child gets older and older, they will see for themselves who was the parent that made the most sacrifices for them and provided them with the most unconditional love… you don't need to drill it in their brain. Just do your job and let the chips fall where they may as time goes along.

The "Potty-Mouth Syndrome" is my description of (PMS). It is a condition that I made up to paint a colorful picture in this chapter to describe a child's behaviors. When I am out

CHAPTER 7: UNDERSTANDING THEIR LANGUAGE

and about, whether at a car wash or a shopping mall, and I hear a young child cursing and using disgusting words in their conversation, the first person I internally blame for that child's actions are his/her parents.

The child who carelessly speaks in this fashion on a regular basis is a child who hears this destructive language on a regular basis. Children don't teach themselves how to speak this way, they learn it from their parents or from the environments in which their parents allow them to be exposed to. Regretfully, this is one of the lessons that I had to learn the hard way.

During my own divorce and child custody hearings, the court oftentimes made rulings that I did not think were fair to my children. Sometimes the decisions made by the court made me very angry... so angry that it sometimes took me days to calm down and accept what the court's ruling was. During my momentary temper-tantrums, I let my speech get the best of me sometimes in front of my kids and, once I finally came to my senses, I felt extremely guilty for having said those things in the presence of my kids. However, the good thing that came out of that experience is that my kids have never been heard repeating any of the choice words that they heard me saying.

In my home, my kids know that I don't talk like that – it's not a true characteristic of who I am as a person. The biggest reason that I do not use that type of language is because I don't even want to be at risk of *accidentally* allowing my kids to hear me talk in a profane manner in *any* situation – and then find out that they have also been using that language. Since I know that I will not always be able to be with my kids 24/7, I must raise them in such a way that I can trust that they will act according to the way I have raised them and trained them when they are in public outside of my presence.

However you want your kids to act and treat others when they are away from you, is how YOU must act when your children are in your presence. As they get older and older, they will eventually end up being a mirror image of you... one way or another.

If you are in favor of the idea that telling your children that your divorce/custody case is not their fault, but just do not know the right way to go about doing it, seek professional help or advice from a licensed mental health specialist for recommendations that may work best for your situation. No matter what advice you are given by your mental health specialist, just keep in mind that what worked for others is not guaranteed to work for your situation.

If you are a parent that can vividly recall the hurt, pain, confusion, anxiety and stress that *you* felt as a child, as a result of your parent's divorce or child custody process, do not buckle YOUR kids into that same emotional rollercoaster. If you can admit to yourself that you did not enjoy the pain and emotional torment that you had to endure as a child, then why would you put your own children through the exact same torment?

If you simply humble yourself to do something different in your life, have an open mind and follow the recommendations and tips in this book, then you may very well be the first person in your family history to be on the road to breaking generational curses and having a much better quality of life for you and your

CHAPTER 7: UNDERSTANDING THEIR LANGUAGE

children.

Even when your child is not physically speaking to you, get into the habit of paying very close attention to his/her body language. Your child's body language and sudden behavior changes are how they speak to you while remaining silent. Understand and know that, even when you think your child is not paying attention to the things you say or the things that you do, they're watching you and listening to you more closely than you may be giving them credit for.

Children in today's society are much smarter and much more advanced than we as adults give them credit for. Do not insult their intelligence by concluding that they have no idea what's going on between you and your co-parent. Always *tell* your children how much you love them. Always *demonstrate* to your children how much you love them. Always make your child feel like they can come to you and talk to you about *anything* that may be bothering them. Always make it clear to your child that you are there to listen to them when they desire to talk about troubling matters. Most importantly, always reassure your children that *their voice matters!*

Mental Rest Area

Now that you have a much better understanding about the languages that your child uses to speak to you, write down a few things in this section that you think your child may be trying to say to you, based on their body language. Also, write down a few things that you feel like you can change in your life to prove to your child that you are very interested in making more time for them to be heard on issues in your co-parenting routine that may be bothering them.

CHAPTER 7: UNDERSTANDING THEIR LANGUAGE

CHAPTER 8

In Times of Need

Prior to the start of your legal separation, divorce or child custody case, were you happily married and living life thinking that you were with the person of your dreams? Prior to the start of your legal separation, divorce or child custody case, were you and your co-parent living together in a **common-law marriage**?[37] Prior to the start of your legal separation, divorce or child custody case, did you and your co-parent bring a child into the world together as a result of a single night of heated passion and lust-driven intimacy?

An online resource, *FindLaw.com*, offers that, "A common law marriage is one in which the couple lives together for a period of time and holds themselves out to friends, family and the community as 'being married,' but without ever going

---

[37] The cohabitation of a couple even when it does not constitute a legal marriage.

through a formal ceremony or getting a marriage license."

No matter what type of colorful wording you choose to describe your relationship, there is one thing that you and your co-parent will always have in common for the remainder of your lives... your child!

Just because you and your co-parent did not legally get married or engage in a common-law marriage arrangement, does not make you **exempt**[38] from ending up in family court. Once you and your co-parent have a child together and decide that you do not want to be in each other's life anymore, you are both still legally and financially responsible for the care, maintenance and welfare of the biological child that you both share.

More than likely, when your relationship was thriving and seemingly going the way you were hoping it would go, each of you shared some favorable benefits. You had someone to help you pay the rent/mortgage to keep a roof over your child's head... you had someone to help you buy groceries for the household so that your child always had food to eat... you had someone to help you contribute to the monthly childcare bills... you had someone to help you pay for your child's clothing needs... and you also had someone to help you pay for recreational sporting activities that allowed your child to do something fun and cater to their active lifestyle. Then, in an unexpected turn of life-events, everything you once had

---

38 To release or deliver from some liability or requirement to which others are subject.

CHAPTER 8: IN TIMES OF NEED

financial help with was now your sole responsibility because your co-parent had abandoned the relationship and no longer felt obligated to contribute.

This is the most common aspect of child custody cases that I despise the most. So many parents around the world adopt the unrealistic mentality that, just because they have fallen out of love with their co-parent, for whatever reasons, they do not have to help that co-parent take care of *their* child. The facts are clear – you *and* your co-parent brought a child into the world who didn't ask to be here and so, therefore, you *and* your co-parent must continue working together to support that child no matter what. Period!

In today's economy, the parent that is granted either *sole custody* or *primary physical custody* has the financial responsibility of ensuring that all of the child's needs are met on a continuous basis. To some parents who are left with only *joint legal custody*, they may not have any financial problems which would hinder their ability to help support their child. On the other hand, if a parent who has joint legal custody does not provide any financial assistance to the other parent, then that is when the parent with sole custody or primary physical custody is left to carry the weight all by themselves.

If you are not very familiar with any of these terms, here is a general description. Please understand that these general descriptions may have other specific terms and conditions attached to them by the family court, as each case has its own set of unique variables.

Sole custody is when the court has given you the sole

authority to make all relative decisions concerning the care and well-being of your child. This includes what school your child will attend, where they will live, decisions regarding what type of medical, dental or mental health treatment your child can take advantage of, as well as what visitation arrangements they would like the court to implement and enforce. Being granted sole custody should be looked upon as a great honor. It means that the court trusts you to make all the right decisions for your child. If the court ever grants you sole custody, guard this privilege with all of your might because, just as quick as the court granted you with this level of custody, the court can also take it away from you if you fail to successfully uphold all of the responsibilities that come along with this title.

Primary physical custody is when you have proven to the court that you have been your child's primary provider or caregiver for most of the child's life. With this custody arrangement, the parent who does *not* have primary physical custody of the child may still be able to have weekly or bi-weekly visitation privileges. These visits can either be every weekend, every other weekend, one weekend per month or any other arrangement that the court deems as being in the best interest of the child. This includes a rotating visitation schedule for each parent during special holidays or summer vacation periods when the child is out of school.

Joint legal custody is when the court grants both parents the equal ability to make legal decisions regarding what's best for the child – on issues such as where the child will go to school and what type of medical care the child should receive. In this

CHAPTER 8: IN TIMES OF NEED

arrangement, there is still only one parent that has primary *physical* custody of the child, but both parents are given joint authority to make relative decisions regarding general and/or specific needs of their child that both parents deem to be in the best interest of their child.

Although there are many parents who are already aware of certain services or resources that are at their disposal when financial hardships arise, there are just as many parents out there who have no idea about the services that are available to help them get through occasional hard times. In this chapter, I am happy to share with you some free or reduced services that may greatly benefit you and your child in your time of need.

Assistance with Rent, Utilities and Clothing

As you may recall from previous chapters, I provided you with some very detailed examples of the risk factors associated with phoning in false or misleading allegations of child abuse or child neglect against your co-parent. Nevertheless, whenever someone calls in to the Child Abuse Hotline to make an allegation of child abuse or child neglect against you, it generates a case number that is eventually assigned to a social worker with the Department of Children and Family Services (DCFS) or Child Protective Services (CPS). Once a case number has been opened up as a result of the reported allegation, that case number will remain open until DCFS or CPS has concluded their investigation and has made a decision as to whether or not the allegations are false or substantiated.

At some point in time, the social worker assigned to your case will usually try to contact you by phone first to set up a date and time to come out to your home to meet with you to discuss the allegation(s). If the social worker is unable to reach you by phone, after a few attempts, he or she will come out to your home to try to meet with you in person. If the social worker is still unable to get in touch with you by popping up at your house, they will usually leave a business card on your front door. If this happens, I highly recommend that you call them immediately upon noticing their business card on your front door. It does not matter if YOU feel like the allegations are false or not, the longer it takes you to call them back the more it can start to look like you have something to hide.

Once DCFS or CPS comes out to your house, there are some critical things that they will be looking for. They want to inspect your house to make sure there is plenty of food in the house for your child to eat… they want to see where your child sleeps in the home… they may want to speak directly to your child to ask them certain questions (outside of your presence)… and they may also want to conduct a cursory examination of your child to prove or disprove any allegations of physical abuse. After speaking to your child, they will then sit you down and ask you questions regarding the allegations that were reported to them. Do not drive yourself up the wall by asking the social worker who called in to report you; they will not tell you! Depending on the circumstances surrounding the type of allegations that were reported, the investigation process can take a few weeks…

CHAPTER 8: IN TIMES OF NEED

a few months or even longer! As long as your case remains open and unresolved, there are some benefits that you may be eligible to receive, although this is not a guarantee in every case. And now... for the part you've been waiting for.

If your social worker feels that you may be eligible for assistance, he or she can get you some financial assistance from the department that will help you pay your rent, buy school clothes for your children, help you pay for childcare or even help you with buying groceries for your household. In some cases, you may also be eligible to get assistance with paying your utilities.

Assistance with these types of benefits typically depends on a few different factors. You may be asked to meet certain eligibility requirements that will determine the amount of assistance available to you. In most cases, this assistance may only be offered to you if DCFS or CPS has enough funding on hand to help you in these areas. Once you make your needs known to your social worker, your social worker can find out if funding is available for open cases in your area. These types of benefits existed for open cases within the County of Los Angeles prior to the COVID-19 pandemic. Based on the economic impact that COVID-19 has had throughout the United States, funding for this type of assistance may or may not be available now.

If your case is still in an open status during the Thanksgiving or Christmas holiday season, DCFS or CPS may also have enough resources to make sure you and your children receive enough food to make sure you have food for the holidays. If they should happen to have an over-abundance of food on hand, there are food banks and other organizations that customarily donate excess food to DCFS and CPS for families in need. If the department does not have enough food to hand out directly to families that are on their case-load, you and your children may receive an invitation from your social worker to attend a coordinated Thanksgiving dinner event that is hosted by a local school or church in your area.

If it is a holiday that you celebrate, it is not uncommon for your social worker to invite you and your children to a Christmas holiday event that will afford you and your children an opportunity to have a nice Christmas dinner and receive Christmas toys as well. If your case is still in an open status prior to the start of your child's school year, DCFS or CPS may also be able to provide your child with a new backpack for school that is loaded with brand new school supplies to make them feel good about being ready for their first day of school. Again, many of these resources and benefits are only available to you if funding is available to the department. Ask your social worker if any of these services can be made available to you and your children.

Once you have been notified by your social worker that you do in fact qualify to receive financial assistance in the areas described above, your social worker can provide you with more information regarding how your financial assistance will be disbursed. In some cases, you will not be given a physical check for the amount of your monthly rent. DCFS or CPS will customarily pay a portion of your rent by giving a check to the leasing office of your apartment complex, or your landlord, and advise them to apply it to your rent.

Don't forget, in order for you to receive any of these benefits to assist you with your financial hardships, your DCFS or CPS case must still be *open*! If you currently have an open case with either DCFS or CPS, ask your social worker for more information about how you and your children can take advantage of any free or reduced services that may be available to you. If you are being represented by a private attorney, ask your attorney to look into these services on your behalf. Do not take it upon yourself to contact DCFS or CPS to inquire about any of these services unless your attorney instructs you to do so.

Additional Resources for Nutrition Benefits

With regard to the resources described in the previous section, those resources apply only to parents who have an active/open case with DCFS or CPS. The benefits described in *this* section are for the co-parent who has either primary physical custody or sole custody of a minor child.

If you have primary physical custody or sole custody of a child under the age of five years old, and are having difficulty with buying enough groceries for your household, it may benefit you to apply for WIC.

Go online and do a Google search for a WIC office in your local area. To be more specific, go to the Google search engine and type in: *WIC office near me* and then activate your search inquiry. Once you have done this, you will see a variety of different search results for WIC locations in your area – starting with the offices that are closest to where you are located at the time of your search.

"Established as a pilot program in 1972 and made permanent in 1974, WIC is administered at the Federal level by the Food and Nutrition Service of the U.S. Department of Agriculture," says an online publication published by *fns.usda.gov*. When the WIC program was first started, it was commonly identified as a program that was put in place for *women*, *infants* and *children*… thus the name WIC. This was largely due to the fact that, back in those days, it was unheard of for fathers to be the ones who had primary physical custody, or even sole custody of minor children. In cases of divorce, legal separation or child custody matters, the children were almost always cared for primarily by the mother.

Fast forward to the 21st century, more and more fathers have been and are still being awarded either primary physical custody or sole custody of their children. In cases where the father is the child's primary caregiver, the father is now able to apply for WIC benefits to help feed his children. If you are a father with either primary physical custody or sole custody of your child, contact your local WIC office to find out how to apply for benefits that will provide food for your child and your household up until your child reaches the age of five years old. If you encounter information online that does not appear to be helpful, or is hard to understand, call your local WIC office to schedule an appointment to speak to a representative who will assist you with applying in-person.

CHAPTER 8: IN TIMES OF NEED

Additional Childcare Resources

With the cost of living continuing to soar to unbearable levels, especially in California, there are scores of parents that are struggling to make ends meet on a monthly basis. Of the recurring monthly expenses at the top of the list for most single parents, childcare is also a major concern. For the co-parent who has primary physical custody or sole custody of a minor child, being able to afford childcare brings about a great deal of stress and elevated anxiety as the beginning of each month approaches.

For the parent who does not have the financial ability to maintain childcare services, it makes it extremely difficult to either find work or keep the job they already have. If you are a parent who is looking to take advantage of more affordable childcare rates, I recommend that you get on your computer and do some online research by looking up subsidized childcare programs that may service your local area. In the majority of circumstances, a subsidized childcare program can pay your childcare provider a large percentage of childcare fees that would usually be paid by you. You must meet the eligibility requirements in order to qualify for these benefits. No matter what your situation is, don't assume that you don't qualify based on what someone else may have told you. Take the necessary steps to see for yourself if you qualify.

Here is a quick example of how a subsidized childcare program will usually operate. If you are a parent residing within the County of Los Angeles, one of the most highly recognized subsidized childcare programs is offered by the Pomona Unified School District Child Development Program (PUSD). The Pomona Unified School District Child Development Program offers a wide variety of childcare services, including certified daycare centers as well as daycare services that are offered in private homes that meet state or county licensing regulations.

If you are a parent who does not have consistent, trustworthy or reliable help to get your child to and from school during your work hours, you would contact the PUSD Child Development Program and tell them that you are looking to obtain before and after school care for your child. Once you successfully go through the screening and application process, and are approved to start your childcare services, you would then be able to take advantage of having before and after school childcare for your child. In this scenario, you would drop your child off at the daycare provider, staff members at that daycare would then drop your child off at school in the morning, pick your child up after school is over and then bring your child back to the daycare facility to wait for you to pick your child up. If approved, having access to before and after school childcare is a blessing in disguise for the parent who is concerned about always being able to get to work on time.

Another popular childcare program for parents residing within the County of Los Angeles is offered by Options for Learning Child Care Services. This is another subsidized childcare program that works similar to the PUSD Child Development Program. For more information on how to apply for either of these subsidized childcare programs, go to the

CHAPTER 8: IN TIMES OF NEED

Google search engine and type in: *PUSD Child Development Program* located in Pomona, California. You can also do a Google search for: *Options for Learning Child Care*. In either search, the first page of search results will prove to be the most reliable information for you to begin researching to get the application process started. For residents living within the County of Los Angeles, these are the most popular childcare programs to apply for.

I highly recommend that you start this process as soon as humanly possible! Sometimes the waiting list to get into these programs can take several weeks up to several months. Due to the COVID-19 pandemic that hit the United States and countless other countries in March of 2020, many of the free or reduced services mentioned in this chapter may or may not still be available. The COVID-19 pandemic has taken an unprecedented toll on the economy for countries all around the globe, including the United States, and the funding that was once available to provide these services to families in need may take a considerable amount of time before the funding to resume these programs has been restored. Don't give up... keep trying.

Reduced Rates for Legal Representation

If you recall from previous chapters, you remember reading about the benefits of having the court grant your *Fee Waiver Application*. Although a granted *Fee Waiver Application* exempts you from having to pay for court filing fees, it does not entitle you to free or discounted services in the event that you need to hire a private attorney to represent you in court. Should you ever stand in need of hiring a private attorney, please understand that hiring a private attorney can be extremely costly, especially if you are already having financial hardships!

Depending on a wide variety of variables, your attorney can charge you whatever fees he/she wants to charge you. Under most circumstances, an attorney's initial retainer fee might depend on the seriousness of why you are looking to hire them in the first place, and not all attorneys are going to charge you the same amount for the same "type" of representation. If you feel like there is just no way for you to avoid having to hire a private attorney, but you want to save yourself some money, NOW is the perfect time to go find a highlighter and make note of these recommendations.

In all of the books that I have written, I always try to use a few personal moments of transparency to help paint brilliant pictures of the things that I've gone through and survived, so that my testimonies can possibly help someone else get through whatever storms they may be experiencing in their own life.

When I initially filed for divorce, I did not have the extra money at my disposal to hire a private attorney. Since I had studied Criminal Justice for most of my high school and college years, I was pretty familiar with courtroom etiquette and a lot of legal terminology. I was always very gifted at reading and writing, and used those gifts throughout my lifetime to help myself and help others. I've always had a fascination with learning how the legal system really works.

CHAPTER 8: IN TIMES OF NEED

When I first began attending a local community college to start working on my degree in Administration of Justice, I ended up taking a class called Report Writing. Based on what I had already learned in high school and the Los Angeles County Sheriff's Department Deputy Explorer Cadet Program, I never even studied for this class and ended up with an A- as my final grade. During my 13 year, intermittent employment in the private security industry many years ago, I earned my first promotion to the position of Corporal during my initial 90-day probationary period. This was the first time that I had ever been offered a promotion while still on probation.

After finally earning another promotion to the position of Sergeant within that same company, I was transferred to work in a more upscale part of town for an office that was being restructured to make improvements in the security department. During my time at my new work location, my staff and I made quite a few arrests. These arrests ranged from *petty theft, fighting* and *trespassing* – all the way up to *grand theft, burglary from motor vehicle, commercial burglary* and *assault with a deadly weapon*. The purpose of arresting people for these types of crimes was to ensure that they were prosecuted and convicted of the crimes that we arrested them for so that they would not come back to our property to commit more crimes without considering the risks. Once we arrested a suspect, as the shift supervisor, I knew it was highly likely that the arrest report that we wrote would eventually make its way to court as evidence.

In my experience over the years, even if the person we arrested was caught red-handed breaking the law, the charges could have been dropped if the District Attorney found that our arrest report lacked factual accounts of the crime, or if our report lacked any other credible information. Since I saw that there was a need, I asked my superiors if I could volunteer my time to come in on my off days and teach a report writing class to my officers for four hours... they gladly approved my request. The company thought that this was such a good idea, after they sat in on my first class, they started paying me for the full four hours, even though I offered to do it for free.

This is the type of knowledge that allowed me to feel confident enough to represent myself throughout my divorce and child custody proceedings. Once again, now would be a good time to pick up that highlighter again and highlight a few nuggets that may help you out in your time of need!

If there comes a time in your divorce or child custody case that you need to hire a private attorney, ask your attorney how much he/she will charge you for Limited-Scope representation. Limited-Scope representation is when an attorney agrees to represent you in court for *one* specific matter. This means that an attorney representing you for an upcoming court hearing will typically only appear in court for you at one or two hearings to argue one or two aspects of your case. If your co-parent is taking you to court to either get your child support increased, get your parenting time with your child reduced or to get spousal support from you, it could be very costly for you to have an attorney to represent you for all three of these matters.

This is the time in your case where you need to decide which matter is the most important matter that you want an attorney

CHAPTER 8: IN TIMES OF NEED

to represent you on. If you want your attorney to fight for you against your co-parent's efforts to make you pay spousal support, then you need to ask your attorney how much he/she will charge you for Limited-Scope representation to argue <u>only</u> spousal support matters. If you want your attorney to fight for you against your co-parent's efforts to take away your parenting time with your child, then you need to ask your attorney how much he/she will charge you for Limited-Scope representation pertaining <u>only</u> to matters regarding your parenting time with your child.

I have always maintained primary physical custody of my children. Once I began to see warning signs that my children's safety and well-being were at risk when they were outside of my presence, I used every possible measure of my legal knowledge and all of my previous experiences to fight for what I felt was best for my children. Even with the amount of experience and knowledge that I already had before filing for divorce, it was not easy by any means.

Keeping my eyes focused on my kids and what was best for them is what got me though the tough times and, just as my kids had learned a lot from me, I learned a lot from them as well. For a laundry list of counter-productive reasons, my divorce and child custody battle took more than four years to finally get resolved. Within that time, I only hired an attorney on two separate occasions. The two attorneys that I hired were for Limited-Scope representation and, throughout all other phases of my family court hearings, I represented myself. Based on all of the things that are itemized in this section, I was ultimately awarded sole custody of my children and we are now simply enjoying our life together.

Although the tips and recommendations in this section can prove to be very helpful to you, while also saving you a great deal of money, they are just suggestions for the purposes of steering you in the right direction. If you are ever in doubt about what you should ultimately do in your own personal legal situation, always consult a credentialed attorney before making any decisions that you think could have an adverse effect on you or your child.

Mental Rest Area

Before moving on to the next chapter, take a few moments to exhale and catch your breath for a moment. After you have given it some deep, honest thought, write down some takeaways that you got from reading this chapter and how this information might be of assistance to you, either now or in the future.

_____
_____
_____
_____
_____
_____
_____

CHAPTER 8: IN TIMES OF NEED

CHAPTER 9

Always Choose Your Child

As you continue on your journey of trying to be the best possible parent that you can be, you are going to fall down, you are going to fail sometimes, you are going to make mistakes, you are going to have moments of smiles and laughter, you will experience moments of great sadness and loss, you are going to be proud of certain choices you've made… and there are other choices that you will make and live to regret, which will hurt you to your core.

At some stage of your life, you have probably heard someone say to you that it is always best to learn from *other people's mistakes* rather than feeling the pain associated with mistakes that you have personally made. As any reasonable person would agree, making the same mistakes over and over and over again is a sign that you are not learning or growing in certain areas of your life. If you are not learning or growing in some of the most critical areas of your own life, then how do you plan on teaching your child how to grow in *their* life as they evolve?

If we can mutually agree that mistakes are going to be made in our lives *anyway*, then it only makes sense that we make different mistakes rather than making the same ones we've already experienced and should have learned from. Making "new" mistakes is a new opportunity for us to show our children that we too are still learning, just as we expect our children to be coachable and learn from us. One of the biggest mistakes that we can make as parents is constantly giving our children the impression that we know it all and that we can do no wrong because we are grown-ups. If it is ever your desire to have your children grow into adulthood and resent you, having this type of mindset is the perfect recipe! However, if you desire to have your children grow into adulthood respecting you for the sacrifices that you made for them, then that is going to require some extreme transparency and humility!

"I sincerely apologize! I should have listened to your feelings rather than *tell you* how to feel."

"I am so sorry for not being there at a time when you were really counting on me to be."

"Please forgive me for not handling that situation better. I will try harder to handle things better next time."

CHAPTER 9: ALWAYS CHOOSE YOUR CHILD

"Please be patient with me as I'm learning how I can be a better parent for you."

"I don't know how to guide you through this challenge you're having in your life, but we will find a way to get through this together."

"I can tell that something is bothering you and I want you to know that I'm here for you in whatever way you need me to be."

"I want you to know that I'm never too busy to listen to you if you need someone to talk to."

"I want you to know that you are the most important person in my life!"

"If there is something that you feel I can be doing better as your parent, I always welcome your thoughts and your ideas because this is really hard work!"

"I am not perfect, and I do not know it all, but I will always teach you what I know about life so that you can always take advantage of the best opportunities."

"I'm not being hard on you to punish you, I'm being hard on you because I love you and I always want to see you win!"

"I am very sorry for coming home and taking my anger and frustrations out on you. I was wrong for that, and I truly apologize!"

"I didn't mean to hurt your feelings and make you feel unimportant. Will you forgive me?"

Now let's be painfully honest here. When was the last time you've made any of these statements to your child? When you are making it a habit of saying these types of things to your child, that's when you know that you are growing into a much more mature level of parenting. In the eyes of your child, you are a leader by default, and a true leader is never afraid to admit when they are wrong or have fallen short on a certain duty or responsibility. You will always be a leader in the eyes of your child, until the day when your child becomes old enough and mature enough to understand what true leadership is supposed to look like.

When you fail to constantly invest your time and energy into developing the life of your child during the early adolescent stages, what you are really doing is forcing them to grow up and figure out life all by themselves. When your child is constantly showing signs that they need love and attention from you, and yet you refuse to give it to them, you are forcing your child to go elsewhere to find the love and attention that they're oftentimes seeking from YOU.

This is the biggest factor in cases where children join gangs

CHAPTER 9: ALWAYS CHOOSE YOUR CHILD

at very young ages. When they are made to feel like they don't matter, or even fit into the fabric of their own families, gangs and other anti-social groups make your child feel like they are a valued part of an alternative family which, in reality, is not a family at all.

In the case of Raymond and Myra, Myra was the parent who willfully chose to put the love of other people and other "things" over the love of her children. Myra was the parent who willfully chose to ignore the psychological and emotional needs of her children. Myra was the parent who willfully chose to turn a blind eye to the fact that her selfishness and her stubbornness are the very traits that caused her to lose everything. Myra was the parent who willfully chose not to participate in the healthy development of her children. Myra was the parent who willfully chose to disobey almost every order that the court made in her family law case. Myra was the parent who willfully chose to make socializing and partying with her friends more of a priority than getting to know her children more and being around to support them. Myra was the parent who willfully chose to risk getting caught by stepping outside of her marriage to pursue what she *thought* was the love of other men who ultimately cared nothing about her.

Whenever Myra went to family court to file a motion, it was always a motion that was geared towards benefitting *Myra*, not her son, Cameron. This was an ongoing practice of hers that allowed the court to see that the well-being and care of her children were not Myra's primary focus. Noticing these patterns displayed by Myra are what likely made the court see that with Raymond was the best place for their son to be.

Water Your Seeds Daily

Imagine that you have enough space in your backyard for a large garden. In this garden, you have every intention on growing some of your favorite fruits and vegetables. Being able to harvest the highest quality crops is a direct result of planting the highest quality seeds in the highest quality soil. Your children are your seeds, and the environments that you expose them to are their soil. If you plant good quality seeds in soil that is contaminated and lacks the proper nutrients, then the good seeds that you planted there will inevitably die or yield a terrible, unhealthy crop. However, if you plant good quality seeds in soil that is also healthy, and does in fact contain an adequate level of nutrition, then the crop that you will eventually harvest will be impressive and plentiful. In theory, your children are no different.

When you allow your children to grow up in places where there is drug abuse, alcohol abuse, gang activity, physical abuse, verbal abuse, mental abuse, emotional abuse or any other counter-productive forms of neglect, up to and including anti-social practices or behaviors, then you are willfully planting your children (your seeds) in the wrong type of soil. When you are regularly exposing your children to people such as law-abiding citizens, highly respected business professionals, people who believe strongly in higher education, people who have long and proven track records of setting goals and

CHAPTER 9: ALWAYS CHOOSE YOUR CHILD

achieving great accomplishments, then you are planting your children (your seeds) in a much higher quality of soil. Just as you were at their age, your children have an extremely high probability of becoming products of their environments.

My *water your seeds* philosophy is something that I created that best describes the individual parent's responsibility to make their children their daily priority and responsibility. So often in our society, parents are so eager to push their children off on friends or family members so that they can run the streets freely without having to worry about the child disrupting their busy social life. So often in our society, parents distance themselves from their children because they are afraid to miss out on all the action and excitement at parties and **amid**[39] the night-life.

Hopefully by now you have already started to identify some things in your particular divorce or child custody situation that you will start doing much differently for the benefit of your child. I hope that this book has shown you the value of choosing the interests and concerns of your child, rather than the interests and concerns of society and your so-called friends. If you find yourself surrounded by friends and family members that encourage you to constantly seek revenge against your co-parent every time something doesn't go your way in court, I am persuaded to believe that you a are surrounding yourself with toxic people who are not even capable of giving you sound, helpful advice.

From this moment forward, start surrounding yourself with

---

39 In or into the middle of; surrounded by; among.

quality people so that your children will have access to quality opportunities. From this moment forward, start surrounding yourself with people who want to see *your children* win so that, by default, you can win also. From this moment forward, surround yourself with people that want to help you find solutions to your life-challenges, rather than create unnecessary problems for you. From this day forward, do not take advice from those who cannot even be responsible enough to control the direction of their own lives... let alone *your* life. From this moment forward, do not allow negative people to dictate to you what you should be doing for your children and how you should be doing it.

Whenever you feel like you are ready to start pursuing a new relationship, let the new person who is trying to become an exclusive part of your life know that NOTHING and NO ONE comes before your children! Let that new person know that having a relationship with you is a "package deal," and that you will not settle for less than that understanding. I also recommend that, before you allow any new relationships to start evolving too soon, you and the new person lay some ground-rules about any expectations you may have.

I am always finding myself strongly encouraging parents to let the new person in their life know up front that their children's opinions and feelings about them carries a lot of weight. By making this known to your new love interest up front, you are potentially saving yourself a great deal of emotional stress later down the line by trying to argue your point *after* something troubling has already happened. If your new love interest gives

CHAPTER 9: ALWAYS CHOOSE YOUR CHILD

off any signs whatsoever that your bond with your children is seemingly going to create an awkward tension between the two of you, then that is probably God trying to warn you that you should be reluctant to continue pursuing a relationship with that person.

If a person doesn't respect and support the bond that you have with your children, at the forefront of a relationship, then they will equally not respect nor support the type of relationship you have with your kids at any other subsequent phase of the relationship either. So many terrible things can go wrong at any given time if you, as a parent, start to develop habits that suggest that you are always siding with your new love interest instead of listening to your child.

The internet has no shortage of statistics that show the disturbing percentages of children who report to their parents that the new boyfriend or girlfriend is abusing them. Sadly, in many cases around the world, the parents oftentimes show more allegiance towards the new boyfriend or girlfriend than they do towards their own children. Being *this* detached from reality, and your parental duties to protect your children, can very easily make your child a target for mental, physical, psychological or even sexual abuse by the new boyfriend or girlfriend. Why would you even want to risk it?

When your children come to you and say that someone is hurting them in some way, choose your children and demonstrate your belief in them. When your children come to you and say that someone has touched them inappropriately, choose your children's word over the word of the person who hurt them. When your children come to you and report to you that someone is constantly bullying them, choose your children's word and let them see that you stand ready and willing to defend them and help them put an end to the bullying.

When your children come to you and tell you that they are scared or afraid, for whatever reason, be there for them by reassuring them that you will never let anything or anyone harm them. No matter how much you think you love the new person in your life, never put that person above the love and adoration of your own child. I am persuaded to believe that there is no greater bond than the bond that a parent has with their child. There's no greater love than the love that a parent has to offer their child. Don't sell your kids out for a new relationship that may very well prove to be over with just as quickly as it got started. Romantic relationships may come and go in your lifetime, but the love between you and your child can last for an eternity if it is planted in the right soil and watered often!

The Coolest Car Game

Before I leave you to ponder all of the tips, suggestions and recommendations that I hope will prove to be of value and benefit to your children, I want to calm your mind and try to help eliminate your anxiety by urging you to start playing *"The Coolest Car Game"* with your children. When my co-parent and I were just beginning to get into our court-ordered visitation routine, I oftentimes felt very afraid to allow our kids to go with her for the weekend or for bi-weekly visits, because of the fact

CHAPTER 9: ALWAYS CHOOSE YOUR CHILD

that her then boyfriend was a thug who I felt was involved in criminal activity.

Since it was no secret that my co-parent's boyfriend and I did not get along under any circumstance, I didn't trust him around my children. Due to the fact that I was always concerned for their safety during their visitations with their mother, I constantly taught them how to protect themselves and stick together while they were outside of my presence. During the ongoing child exchanges that took place at the start and end of each weekend or bi-weekly visit with the children, I started to take notice that the children's mother was always driving different kinds of cars. I thought it was very suspicious that, within the period of about one year, the children's mother had been seen driving the kids around in two or three different types of cars.

Fearing that my children may one day *not* be returned to me at the end of their weekend visitation, I taught them a game that I referred to as *"The Coolest Car Game."* In this game, I taught my children how to identify the makes and models of a wide range of vehicles in case they ever needed to tell the authorities what type of car a person was driving that tried to take them away against their will or hurt them.

On the days that we spent a lot of time on the road, I noticed that the children were fascinated with muscle cars. Whenever they heard the sound of a loud engine nearby, or approaching us, the kids were sitting up in their seats – looking out of their window to try to find the car that was revving its engine loudly. Once they found it, they would often ask me, "Dad, what kind of car is that?" I saw that as a great opportunity to teach them how to identify cars. Little did they know, I was teaching them how to identify a potential suspect's car if anyone were to ever try to harm them and try to suddenly drive away in an effort to avoid getting caught.

The easiest car to teach them how to identify was a Ford Mustang. Whenever we pulled up near a Ford Mustang, I trained their eyes to focus on the horse emblem on the front of the car. I would always tell them, "Whenever you see a car that has a horse on the front of it, that means the car is a Ford Mustang; all you have to remember is what color it is." Another car that was easy for them to identify was the Audi. Whenever we saw a car that had the four silver circles on the front and rear of the car, they knew that car was an Audi. The next type of car that I taught them how to identify was the Chevy Corvette. "Whenever you see a car that looks like it has a crooked cross on the front and back, it's a Chevy Corvette. Chevy has a lot of different models, but the Chevy Corvette is one of the fastest cars ever," I would excitedly share with them. Other common cars that I taught my children how to identify are: Nissan, Lexus, Porsche, Maserati, Mercedes and BMW. When I first began teaching my children how to identify various makes and models of vehicles, they were only five years old. By the time they were about six or seven years old, they were able to identify nearly every car that was driving on the streets, without hesitation!

You may think of this type of game as being a bit "cheesy" or "corny" but, if your child is ever put in harm's way by any person who attempts to abduct them or take them against their will, you would be extremely grateful and proud of your child

CHAPTER 9: ALWAYS CHOOSE YOUR CHILD

for being able to tell the police what type of car the "bad guy" was driving... and ultimately see the person who tried to harm them get put behind bars where they belong.

<u>Exercise #2</u>

As you are driving around town with your children in the car with you, start teaching them how to play *"The Coolest Car Game."* Start off by teaching them how to identify the cars that you think they will remember the most, once they see the car a second or third time. Do not make the game seem too serious or too complex. Make the game seem as easy and as fun as possible. When you pick out a random vehicle and ask your children to try and figure out what kind of car it is, reward them with something special if they get it right. Start off by simply giving them a lot of praise and affirmation.

As they get better at the game and are starting to identify more and more vehicles, reward them by taking them out for pizza, ice cream or even taking them to the store and allowing them to pick out their favorite snack. However you choose to play the game with your kids, just make it fun so that they will want to keep playing. Little do you know, your child being able to identify the car of a bad person who's trying to hurt them, may possibly save another child's life.

Because Myra's feelings and ego were so badly bruised by the fact that Raymond had filed for divorce, many of the things she did after the divorce filing were done because her primary focus was getting revenge against Raymond. Raymond, on the other hand, did the total opposite of Myra. Instead of spending years and years of his life trying to get even with Myra, Raymond decided to be a devoted father who made it a habit of telling Cameron that he did nothing wrong to cause the separation between he and Myra; he was not the reason why life was so different now.

Although she could never be convinced of these facts, her bitterness and her anger towards her reality was ultimately the **demise**[40] of everything that she thought was worth fighting for. Little did she know, the universe was about to give her the full return on her investments! When all was said and done, Myra had lost EVERYTHING… including all custody rights for all of her children. When Myra lost custody of the biological child that she and Raymond shared (Cameron), she also lost custody of her child that she already had from her previous relationship (Angelica). At the time Myra had lost her custody rights, Angelica was 13 years old and ended up going to live with her grandparents who lived out of state.

I want to take this last opportunity to paint you a brilliant, mental picture that I never want you to forget.

For just a few moments, I want you to imagine that *your* parent is a basketball coach for a community youth league that you are trying out for. Your parent's job is to pick the best players in attendance so that he/she can put together a strong team of winners. As your parent begins to select the players he/she wants for his/her team, you notice that your parent has

---

40 Death.

CHAPTER 9: ALWAYS CHOOSE YOUR CHILD

picked everyone except for you. As there is only room for one more player on the team, you notice that your parent selects your best friend instead of choosing you.

How would it make you feel to know that your parent saw you standing there waiting to be chosen but, instead, your parent chose your best friend instead of you? If we can mutually agree that this would leave *you* feeling terrible and unworthy of being valued, then that is exactly how your child feels when you choose a new boyfriend or girlfriend rather than choosing to love your own child. There will never be a suitable replacement for your child so, when faced with the task of choosing, always choose your child!

I would like to leave you with an original poem that I wrote entitled, *"Water My Seeds."* This poem was featured in a book that I wrote back in May of 2011 entitled, *"No Longer Silent – By Way of Poetry."*

I would like to impose a question to you
that has been troubling me for far too long,
all I'm asking is that you help me continue my legacy
and water my seeds when I'm gone.
Be very careful because these seeds are extremely precious
and they will mature to be Soldiers like me.
Be patient, as they will make bad choices and mistakes;
observe them from a distance so they can feel like they're free.
Teach them to always be the cream of the crop
regardless of how others will grow,
and how to stand tall through all the gusty winds
and anything else that you think they should know.

THEIR VOICE MATTERS

If they ever get stuck in "The System"
for forcefully taking their enemy's pulse,
even the advice of their most educated mentors
won't help them to escape the end result!
Prepare them for survival, but arm them with intellect,
condition their minds to be as lethal as weapons.
Remind them that backstabbers exist almost everywhere,
even church members can be no exception!
Tell them about faith and the benefits of eternal salvation,
not to mention the importance of renewing their minds.
Keep them surrounded by love and constant support
when true friends and good jobs will seem hard to find.
My main concern is that they're grounded in the Word of the Lord
so that they always have a solid foundation.
Teach them from the beginning to emerge as leaders,
so their lives aren't dependent on employment plantations.
I realize that you also have a life of your own
and that your family has issues and needs,
but if our friendship ever meant what you said that it meant,
when time permits… please water my seeds!

Dedication

This book is dedicated to my two amazing children. Just as I have taught you many important lessons in life, you both have taught me some very important lessons as well. I want to publicly thank you both for the many sacrifices that you have made, which have allowed me to be able to continue pursuing my passion of writing books that educate, empower, uplift and heal those in our society that feel forgotten. As you continue your individual journeys in this life, always know that, even when I failed and made mistakes along the way, my goal is and was always to be the type of father to you that I never had. I thank you for your willingness to forgive me every time I asked you to, and for your unconditional love through the years. I appreciate you both more than you will ever know, and I hope and pray that we will continue to strengthen and maintain the unbreakable bond that we share with one another. Never be afraid to fail in your life, because failure is an important part of success. Never stop setting goals... never stop believing in yourself... never stop supporting one another... never let anyone else in society tell your story... never be a follower... never be afraid to stand on your beliefs... never be discouraged when something you want does not go your way... and never forget the life-lessons that I have always taught you about integrity, leadership and survival. Both of you have so much to offer to the world and I want you to know that you do not have to do it all alone – God and I will be by your side every step of the way. I love you both until the end of time!

This book is also dedicated to children all around the world who find themselves stuck in the middle of unresolved grown-up problems and issues that have nothing to do with them. This book is dedicated to children all over the globe who are the most innocent victims of separation, divorce and child custody matters. *Their Voice Matters* is tangible evidence that the preservation of our children's childhood, mental health, physical well-being and future opportunities need to be of the utmost importance to each and every parent. As parents, we ought not shew our children away from us like annoying flies at a picnic; it is our job and daily responsibility to demonstrate to them how much we cherish them and how much they mean to us.

Our children are the purest form of righteousness that we could ever hope to be within ourselves... until we as parents infect their minds by teaching them toxic behaviors that are only setting them up for failure.

DEDICATION

To All Children: You are special, you are valuable, you are appreciated, you are intelligent, you are wanted, you are needed, you are talented, you are gifted, you are brilliant, you are loved, you are missed, you are worthy of greatness and you are *not* to blame for the mistakes or failures of your parents. When it feels like no one wants to hear how you feel... when you feel like nothing you do is ever enough... when you start to feel sad that no one seems to welcome your ideas... when it seems like your friends and family members have let you down... when you feel like there's no one else in the world who is on your side... whenever you are told to stay in your lane and be quiet, always remember that *"your voice matters!"*

Citations & References

Quote Catalog. (July 4, 2020). *Hurt People Hurt People*. Retrieved from https://quotecatalog.com/quote/yehuda-berg-hurt-people-hur-81z4MNp

Child Welfare Information Gateway. (2019). *Penalties for False Reporting*. Retrieved from https://www.childwelfare.gov/pubPDFs/report.pdf

Find Law. (April 3, 2019). *What is Common Law Marriage: A Definition*. Retrieved from https://family.findlaw.com/marriage/common-law-marriage.html

Fns.usda.gov. (10/10/2013). *More About WIC:* Retrieved from https://www.fns.usda.gov/wic/about-wic-wics-mission#:~:text=Established%20as%20a%20pilot%20program,the%20U.S.%20Department%20of%20Agriculture.

Integrity. (n.d.). In Merriam-Webster.com dictionary. Retrieved from https://www.merriam-webster.com/dictionary/integrity

Dysfunctional. (n.d.). In Merriam-Webster.com dictionary. Retrieved from https://www.merriam-webster.com/dictionary/dysfunctional

One-Up. (n.d.). In Merriam-Webster.com dictionary. Retrieved from https://www.merriam-webster.com/dictionary/one-up

Rest Area. (n.d.). In Merriam-Webster.com dictionary. Retrieved from https://www.merriam-webster.com/dictionary/rest%20area

Debonair. (n.d.). In Merriam-Webster.com dictionary. Retrieved from https://www.merriam-webster.com/dictionary/debonair

Eye Candy. (n.d.). In Merriam-Webster.com dictionary. Retrieved from https://www.merriam-webster.com/dictionary/eye%20candy

Compromised. (n.d.). In Merriam-Webster.com dictionary. Retrieved from https://www.merriam-webster.com/dictionary/compromised

Introvert. (n.d.). In Merriam-Webster.com dictionary. Retrieved from https://www.merriam-webster.com/dictionary/introvert

Standoffish. (n.d.). In Merriam-Webster.com dictionary. Retrieved from https://www.merriam-webster.com/dictionary/standoffish

Blissful. (n.d.). In Merriam-Webster.com dictionary. Retrieved from https://www.merriam-webster.com/dictionary/blissful

Recurring. (n.d.). In Merriam-Webster.com dictionary. Retrieved from https://www.merriam-webster.com/dictionary/recurring

Evidentiary. (n.d.). In Merriam-Webster.com dictionary. Retrieved from https://www.merriam-webster.com/dictionary/evidentiary

Allegiance. (n.d.). In Merriam-Webster.com dictionary. Retrieved from https://www.merriam-webster.com/dictionary/allegiance

Disposition. (n.d.). In Merriam-Webster.com dictionary. Retrieved from https://www.merriam-webster.com/dictionary/disposition

Petitioner. (n.d.). In Merriam-Webster.com dictionary. Retrieved from https://www.merriam-webster.com/dictionary/petitioner

Respondent. (n.d.). In Merriam-Webster.com dictionary. Retrieved from https://www.merriam-webster.com/dictionary/respondent

Infidelity. (n.d.). In Merriam-Webster.com dictionary. Retrieved from https://www.merriam-webster.com/dictionary/infidelity

Allegations. (n.d.). In Merriam-Webster.com dictionary. Retrieved from https://www.merriam-webster.com/dictionary/infidelity

Mediation. (n.d.). In Merriam-Webster.com dictionary. Retrieved from https://www.merriam-webster.com/dictionary/mediation

Proof of Service. (n.d.). In Merriam-Webster.com dictionary. Retrieved from https://www.merriam-webster.com/legal/proof%20of%20service

Process Server. (n.d.). In Merriam-Webster.com dictionary. Retrieved from https://www.dictionary.com/browse/process-server

Malicious. (n.d.). In Merriam-Webster.com dictionary. Retrieved from https://www.merriam-webster.com/dictionary/malicious

Crucify. (n.d.). In Merriam-Webster.com dictionary. Retrieved from https://www.merriam-webster.com/dictionary/crucify

Admonish. (n.d.). In Merriam-Webster.com dictionary. Retrieved from https://www.merriam-webster.com/dictionary/admonish

Shenanigans. (n.d.). In Merriam-Webster.com dictionary. Retrieved from https://www.merriam-webster.com/dictionary/shenanigans

Leniencies. (n.d.). In Merriam-Webster.com dictionary. Retrieved from https://www.merriam-webster.com/dictionary/leniencies#synonyms

Empathy. (n.d.). In Merriam-Webster.com dictionary. Retrieved from https://www.merriam-webster.com/dictionary/empathy

Substantiated. (n.d.). In Merriam-Webster.com dictionary. Retrieved from https://www.merriam-webster.com/dictionary/substantiated

Adoration. (n.d.). In Merriam-Webster.com dictionary. Retrieved from https://www.merriam-webster.com/dictionary/adoration

Compelled. (n.d.). In Merriam-Webster.com dictionary. Retrieved from https://www.merriam-webster.com/dictionary/compelled

Sporadically. (n.d.). In Merriam-Webster.com dictionary. Retrieved from https://www.merriam-webster.com/dictionary/sporadically

Inconclusive. (n.d.). In Merriam-Webster.com dictionary. Retrieved from https://www.merriam-webster.com/dictionary/inconclusive

Unfounded. (n.d.). In Merriam-Webster.com dictionary. Retrieved from https://www.merriam-webster.com/dictionary/unfounded

Due Process. (n.d.). In Merriam-Webster.com dictionary. Retrieved from https://www.merriam-webster.com/dictionary/due%20process

Utter. (n.d.). In Merriam-Webster.com dictionary. Retrieved from https://www.merriam-webster.com/dictionary/utter

Incorrigible(n.d.). In Merriam-Webster.com dictionary. Retrieved from. https://www.merriam-webster.com/dictionary/incorrigible

Common-Law Marriage. (n.d.). In Merriam-Webster.com dictionary. Retrieved from https://www.merriam-webster.com/dictionary/common-law%20marriage

Exempt. (n.d.). In Merriam-Webster.com dictionary. Retrieved from https://www.merriam-webster.com/dictionary/exempt

Amid. (n.d.). In Merriam-Webster.com dictionary. Retrieved from https://www.merriam-webster.com/dictionary/amid

Demise(n.d.). In Merriam-Webster.com dictionary. Retrieved from https://www.merriam-webster.com/dictionary/demise

Our Family Wizard
https://www.ourfamilywizard.com/

Talking Parents
https://talkingparents.com/home

PUBLISHER DISCLAIMER/ADMONISHMENT:
Although we do not present this publication as a substitute for professional legal representation, we do in fact find this book to be a valuable resource for co-parents who are clients of the following agencies and/or organizations: Child Protective Services, Department of Children and Family Services, Family Counseling Services, Marriage and Family Therapists, Family Court [Petitioner & Respondent], Divorce Education, Co-Parenting Programs and Child Development Programs.